Basic Teacher Skills
Revised Edition

Basic Teacher Skills

Handbook for Church School Teachers

Revised Edition

Richard E. Rusbuldt

Judson Press ® Valley Forge

Basic Teacher Skills: Handbook for Church School Teachers
Revised Edition
© 1997 Judson Press, Valley Forge, PA 19482-0851

Bible quotations in this volume are from the NEW REVISED STANDARD VERSION of the Bible, copyrighted 1989 by the Division of Christian Education of the National Council of the Churches of Christ in the United States of America, and are used by permission.

Library of Congress Cataloging-in-Publication Data

Rusbuldt, Richard E.
    Basic teacher skills : handbook for church school teachers / Richard E. Rusbuldt. — Rev. ed.
        p. cm.
    Includes bibliographical references.
    ISBN 0-8170-1255-9 (pbk. : alk. paper)
    1. Christian education—Teaching methods. I. Title.
BV1534.R78 1997
    268'.6—dc21   96-37266

Printed in the U.S.A.
05 04 03 02 01 00 99 98 97
10 9 8 7 6 5 4 3 2

Contents

Preface

Most of you who study this book are considering a commitment to volunteering as a teacher in the Sunday church school of your local church.[1] Teaching is ministry. Teachers are partners with God in the nurture and growth of the people of God. For many decades, the church has depended on volunteer teachers, such as you, to communicate its history and its message. This is a great calling—the ministry of teaching.

You enter the volunteer teaching ranks at a most significant time in the history of the church school. Volunteer teachers, more than any other leaders, can impact the church school of the year 2000 and beyond. Will the Sunday school, using volunteer teachers, be able to function in the future as a valid and effective educational ministry? The answer to this question is an unqualified yes. There is no other way, and besides, this is the right way. Each of you who teach has a faith, a story, a heritage to share. God never intended for you to keep it to yourself . . . it is to be given away. The strength of the Christian movement is telling God's story, the Good News of Jesus Christ, the gospel as it is lived out in the lives of individual Christians.

The school as we have known it up to now is at a crossroads. Which way should it go? Should it "close shop" and sink into oblivion? Or can it identify contemporary needs and respond to these needs in creative and meaningful ways? You who teach will help provide the answers to these questions. There was a day when the church school seemed to thrive and grow effortlessly. That day is gone. You enter the ministry of teaching at a time when changing attitudes, needs, and lifestyles call for a more effective approach to the church's educational mission. In some places, this can be accomplished through the currently existing structure and organization. In others, it will require a complete redesign of the educational system of the local church. In either case, effective teachers will still provide the heart of the teaching ministry.

Evaluation of many church schools produces findings that are less than satisfactory and, in some cases, undesirable. Attendance has declined for many years, although there is some evidence indicating that some churches have been able to reverse the decline. Fewer and fewer financial resources are being made available to many schools, yet many church members still expect them to do what they did twenty years ago. Well-trained teachers are usually effective teachers. Effective teachers can provide meaningful educational experiences for all ages and thereby provide a solid base on which to move into the future. You, the volunteer teacher, are one important key to the teaching ministry of the future.

This book will provide you with basic knowledge, tools, and skills for effective teaching. It will also set high standards for you to meet. Some leaders say we cannot ask too much of today's volunteers, especially teachers in the church school. I would respond by suggesting that we have not asked enough. But this book does not just set expectations for you; it also provides you with guidance and help in meeting those expectations. We want you, the beginning teacher, to get a good start in your teaching ministry. Have confidence in the fact that over a period of time you will not only understand and utilize the content of this book but you will also go far beyond these expectations.

For many churches, the church school does have a future, but churches will not discover that future without making a major investment of time and resources in identifying needs and devising effective responses to those needs. You, the beginning teacher, are a part of that effort. If you, the teacher, along with other Christian education leaders in your church, are willing to invest in and plan for the future, then there is a great future ahead for the church's ministry in the church school. If your situation demands it, be bold and creative as you move into "uncharted territory." You will also find that the usefulness of what is shared with you in this book extends beyond the Sunday morning time slot. God is present with you as you move forward. I invite you to pursue this book with vigor and join in building an effective church school for God's people.

Note

1. "Sunday school," "church school," "Sunday church school," and the "church's school" are terms used in various places at one time or another to refer to the church's regular, graded educational program. For consistency, "church school" is the primary term used in this book.

Chapter 1

The Challenge of Teaching and What You Bring to It

Welcome aboard! You are entering the ranks of the most unusual volunteer teaching movement in the world. You are joining with millions of persons who regularly teach the gospel of Jesus Christ in one of the most unique volunteer movements in history.

It began in England as the Sunday school movement (1780) and continues today under a variety of names, including the Sunday church school, the church school, and so forth. Even though the Sunday school originated over two hundred years ago, most church leaders believe that an organized program of Christian teaching still has a significant place in the life of local congregations. Whatever form the program may take in the years that lie ahead, *an effective teacher* will be the *most significant* person in the ministry of teaching.

Teaching is a unique pursuit. Christian teachers accept a significant challenge that includes self-discovery, personal learning and growth, teaching others, meeting the needs of others, excitement, and satisfaction. Each teacher brings what he or she has to offer to the teaching/learning experience and joins hands with God and others to provide quality Christian education.

The Importance of Teaching

Whether your class is large or small, young or old, whether you teach on Sunday morning or on a weekday, you are carrying out

Christ's call: "teaching them to obey everything that I have commanded you" (Matthew 28:20). The teacher's task is very important. Here are some of the reasons.

1. God and teachers are partners—members of the same team. Throughout history, God has called believers to be interpreters of God's revelation. Teaching is one method of interpretation, and it is a high calling.

If you were bowling on a team that was trying to win the league championship, you'd want to have the best bowlers in the league on your team. If you were a pitcher for a softball team contending for a title, you'd like to have a very good catcher and superior fielders who could catch the balls that batters managed to hit. There's something *good* about being on a *good* team. A person's confidence and ability are greatly strengthened when he or she is able to play, work, and team up with quality persons.

You do not teach alone. Keep in mind that God and you are on the same team. You have every right to be confident in this partnership, since the purpose of your school and the teaching ministry of your church is rooted in God. God is the Author of all that Christian teaching is about. The focus of your teaching is the revelation of God in writing (the Bible), in a person (Jesus Christ), and through the presence of the Holy Spirit. Confidently claim God as your partner in teaching because God has promised to be with you as you teach. Matthew 28:20 states, "And remember, I am with you always. . . ." A teacher who had good feelings about her team relationship with God once wrote, "God and I together make a great team . . . little wonderful me, and a great big wonderful God!"

2. According to the apostle Paul, the spiritual gift of teaching is equal to the gifts of preaching, evangelizing, caring, and shepherding. Ephesians 4:11 proclaims that "the gifts he gave were that some should be apostles, some prophets, some evangelists, some pastors and teachers." Jesus spent most of his three years of ministry as a teacher. Assisting others to understand the meaning of the Bible, to develop their faith, and to apply what they believe to everyday life is a supreme calling. Think highly of what you have been called to be—a Christian teacher.

3. Every teacher is in a unique position to influence others for

good and for God. Think for a moment of the exciting possibilities. Jesus chose twelve "raw recruits" whom he taught to be his disciples through a variety of methods. You can read the story of their calling in Mark 1:16-20. The influence of the master Teacher never left their lives. Today's teachers have many opportunities to influence others. Much concern is expressed today over negative influences in the lives of children, youth, and adults. Christian teachers are needed to provide a positive, meaningful Christian influence in the lives of others.

Influencing people is like planting seeds. When a seed is planted, tremendous forces go to work to bring forth germination, growth, and fruit. Teaching is much the same. Teachers sow a variety of seeds in many kinds of soil, some of which, under the guidance of the Holy Spirit, will bring forth life (growth) and fruit (results). Read Jesus' parable of the sower in Mark 4:1-9.

Gardeners are often surprised at what results from their work. One of our recent fall seasons remained warm much longer than usual. On the first day of October, when most people in our area were closing their gardens, I decided to plant some radish, lettuce, and carrot seeds I'd bought at the bargain price of ten cents per packet. As October went by, the young plants were watered by fall rains and grew vigorously, undaunted by a few mild frosts. By mid-November, many of the Early Globe radishes measured nearly three inches across. The white icicle radishes were almost a foot long, and the lettuce was big and crisp! The carrots continued to grow, even in December. As Jesus pointed out, results can vary depending on conditions. One of the teacher's tasks is to provide the best "growing" conditions for students in a limited amount of time.

Some seeds take root and grow quickly, while others die. Still others take a long time to sprout. Teachers not only sow seeds but also cultivate the plant and soil in order to increase growth possibilities. There is also weeding to be done. Plants (learners) need energetic gardeners (teachers) to promote their growth and development. Ultimately, however, growth is the responsibility of the Holy Spirit; the teacher's task is to plant and to cultivate.

4. It's important to understand your students' needs for what they

really are—a challenge and an opportunity to help them, not a threat to you. Each learner has different needs, and each one presents his or her own challenge. One of the teacher's tasks is to discover the challenge presented by each learner—and to respond.

5. Personal growth is exciting too. *Each teacher is a learner.* Most teachers will tell you that the person who learns most from teaching is the teacher! I personally have found this to be true and have experienced the stimulation that comes from learning while teaching. Personal growth and development are extremely important and are often suggested in Scripture. Ephesians 4:15 states, "But speaking the truth in love, we must *grow up* in every way into him who is the head, into Christ" (italics added). In 2 Peter 3:18 we read, "But *grow* in the grace and knowledge of our Lord and Savior Jesus Christ" (italics added). Other relevant verses include 2 Corinthians 9:10; 1 Thessalonians 3:12; Hebrews 6:1; and 1 Peter 2:2. These Scriptures suggest that we are to mature in our faith and grow as persons. This suggests change. Consider possibilities for growth and change. Don't permit them to threaten you. Change can be most meaningful when it is understood. You too will grow and change as you teach and learn. Look forward with anticipation to what happens to you as you grow in your Christian faith and in your ability to teach.

Teaching with Enthusiasm

We have used the word "exciting" several times in this discussion, but the reality is that excitement and enthusiasm have disappeared from a lot of church schools. Many students describe their experience as "boring." In order to reverse this trend, more attention needs to be focused on the role of the teacher. Enthusiasm begins with the teacher. Enthusiasm is a radiant, vibrant, rejuvenating personal quality that attracts other people. Enthusiasm can be cultivated—enthusiasm breeds enthusiasm—and there are many ways teachers can develop it. Interest and an insatiable curiosity develop enthusiasm. The more you learn about your teaching, your class, and your goals, the more excited and enthusiastic you will become. Using different methods in your teaching brings freshness to the class as well as anticipation and enthusiasm for teacher and student alike. As new members come into your class, you will discover that each person brings his or her own enthusiasm and excitement.

It's exciting to plan a session and see things happen the way you planned. It's also satisfying (and humbling) to realize that often more happens than you dreamed could happen. Moments like this occur because God is actively involved in your telling of God's story. God is at work through your teaching.

Nevertheless, things do go wrong sometimes. You will find that some sessions just don't happen the way they were planned. You will experience disappointment and discouragement from time to time. When you have experienced a disappointing class session and survived (you will!), try to discover what went wrong. Then go back to the "drawing board" for the next session. This process will have its exciting moments. When we learn from our mistakes or a difficult experience, we are growing.

Our model teacher is Jesus. Being with Jesus must have been exciting. His teaching produced some remarkable results. He was enthusiastic about the kingdom of God, even though it meant a cross for him. Yet not everyone who listened to Jesus became his follower. These disappointments, however, did not keep Jesus from his mission—redemption and new life for the world. He kept right on teaching!

Each person who responds to the call to be a teacher of the gospel of Jesus Christ brings a wealth of resources and potential to the position. No matter how limited your knowledge of the Christian faith or your experience in the Christian life, you still have the potential to be an effective teacher. If you question your ability to teach, consider the persons Jesus chose to be disciples. Several were rough, unschooled fishermen, while another was a tax collector. All were everyday people like you and me. On paper, they didn't have many credentials for discipleship, but look what happened! The Christian movement today (of which you and I are a part) is the direct result of the disciples' early work as teachers and leaders for Christ in their world. We have a lot to be enthusiastic about!

To Tell the Story

We have a story to tell—God's story. That story, of God's work in a particular period of history, is primarily recorded in the Old and New Testaments. Even as a coin has two sides, the story has two dimensions. On one side, there is the actual account of the story as found in the Bible. Gabriel Fackre in his book *The Christian Story*[1] refers to the "acts in the Christian drama" as being Creation, Fall, Covenant, Christ, Church, Salvation, Consummation—with their Prologue and Epilogue, God. For most Christians, these are the key steps in the story.

On the other side of the coin is your personal experience with the biblical account of God's story. What impact has God's revelation made in your life? What has changed because of your faith in Jesus Christ? What has happened to you since you joined the ranks of "those people called Christians"? This is "your story" about God's story. Together, they sum up the experiences that you bring to the teacher's role and task.

You are basically a storyteller. The story you tell is about God, creation, and all the relationships God has with what God created. The rest of the story consists of what has happened to you as a result of God's story. The very fact that you have agreed to teach indicates that God's story has made its impact on your life. This story is so great that you must teach! You want it to change and strengthen the lives of others.

Peter wanted to be a fisherman. He loved to fish, didn't mind the long hours or rough conditions, and looked forward every day to the full boat he might bring home. Then Jesus asked him to become a part of God's story. So Peter gave up his nets and began to live out the story. (Read Mark 1:16-21.)

As a boy, I loved the farm. I worked on farms during the summer and spent as much time at my grandmother's farm as possible. I still love to grow things. I have a big garden and a greenhouse that I maintain year round. But God's story wouldn't allow me to live out my life as a farmer.

You've just read Peter's story and mine. What is yours? Your story will be different from the stories of the people you teach, even as it differs from Peter's and mine. But what God's story has done in our lives is "shareable" and is to be communicated as part of our telling of the story.

Jesus came to us as part of God's unfolding story, but we rejected him. In fact, we put the Storyteller to death. But such a story could not be kept in a tomb. The glory of Easter Sunday's explosion into life remains with us today. This is the story we have to tell—shaped by our experiences with God's story.

What Do You Bring to Teaching?

What strengths do you bring to teaching? New, inexperienced teachers tend to worry about such things as lack of experience, limited knowledge of the Bible, lack of time, and inability to plan. Any or all of these may be very real but should not overshadow the very real resources and strengths that you bring to your role.

When you think positively about yourself, what resources do you see? Make a list of the strengths and skills you bring to the task of teaching. Write out commitment and faith statements that describe yourself. The following categories and examples may help you begin this process.

Some of my strengths are:
(Example: I meet people easily; I don't get nervous in front of a group.)

Some skills I bring to teaching are:
(Example: I know how to operate a VCR; I can tell a story.)

The commitments I bring to teaching are:
(Example: I'm willing to take the time to do a good job; I'm committed to team teaching.)

My personal faith is:
(Example: Strong, growing, new, or something I want to share.)

As you analyze your strengths, skills, commitments, and personal faith, it is also important to recognize inadequacies you may bring to teaching. Each of us has weaknesses as well as strengths and gifts. Each inadequacy can become a future personal growth target. Make a list of personal growth areas.
Areas in which I need and hope to grow include:
(Example: Bible knowledge; a strong prayer life, etc.)

Now consider the question, Which growth area needs my attention first? Where do you need to begin? For instance, if the lack of Bible knowledge is a major concern, could you begin to respond to this need by a thorough reading of the four Gospels? Or if you wish to develop a strong personal prayer life, could you obtain pointers from someone who does have a strong prayer life? It is not too early to make decisions about addressing some of the personal teaching needs you have listed.

Your Feelings about Teaching

Are you excited about the prospect of teaching even though you may feel somewhat nervous? If you have already started to teach, are you enthusiastic? If you find teaching to be exciting, you will most likely have a good experience, regardless of your limited knowledge or experience. Your attitude toward teaching is very important. It will directly affect your preparation, classroom presence, and the response of the students in your class. An underlying attitude of anticipation and excitement will help carry you through the learning period when successes and failures may be mixed and puzzling.

Teachers of many years' experience still have disappointments as well as successes—we all do. Experienced teachers, however, have learned to accept disappointments as part of the teaching/learning experience. Jesus was disappointed when the rich young ruler walked away that night, unable to make the key decision he should have made. But Jesus didn't give up. New teachers tend to let disappointing experiences become "mountains" rather than "molehills" and aren't ready to accept disappointments.

How do you rate *your feelings* about teaching? On the scale below, ten represents the highest, and one, the lowest feelings you have about teaching. Where would you place yourself on the scale? Mark an *X* where you think you are right now.

How do I feel about teaching?

1	5	10
"I'm scared!"	"So-so"	"I can't wait to begin!"

If you placed your *X* between five and ten on the scale, you'll probably have little difficulty with your feelings and attitudes. If you placed it below five, you may want to do one of two things. Go ahead and teach and see if your feelings change, or talk about your feelings with the person who asked you to teach.

At the end of your first month of teaching, come back to the scale and locate yourself again. Have your feelings and attitudes changed? If so, in which direction? Ask yourself if you are satisfied with where you are on the scale. Do the same thing after your third month of teaching and again after the sixth month. Keep in touch with your feelings.

Facts and Feelings

Some churches and their teachers approach teaching with the thought that sharing content (facts) is the main goal of teaching. This assumption stems from understanding the Bible as a book of facts to be communicated (taught) as history, facts, details, and stories. It is true that there is important content to be shared. However, content cannot be effectively shared without full recognition of the importance of feelings and relationships.

Your feelings about each person in your class are crucial to the learning experience. Your feelings toward the class or group, your coteacher, your church, your community, your students' parents, God, and yourself are all vital parts of teaching. Although it isn't necessary to do a complete analysis of your feelings every week, it is important to get in touch with your own feelings from time to time, as well as those of your class or group.

Be sure to recognize each person in your class as an individual toward whom you have personal feelings. Likewise, each person in your class has feelings toward you. You will also have feelings about the class as a group, and the class as a group will have feelings toward you.

It is helpful to be aware of these different feelings. For instance, it is normal for most teachers to have warm feelings for those children who are well behaved, cooperative, and generally pleasant. The child who is cantankerous, nervous, disruptive, emotionally volatile, or "antsy" can be difficult to teach and can elicit negative feelings.

Teachers of adult classes usually have warm feelings toward adults who participate in discussions, are generally helpful, and attend regularly. Adults who refuse to participate or attend infrequently usually elicit different feelings. You will find it difficult to have warm, positive feelings about any person in your class who makes teaching difficult for you and the class.

The most important step in dealing with your feelings is to be aware of them. The teacher who is aware of his or her own feelings and can change or modify those feelings when necessary will be most effective in relating to persons in the class.

It is not wrong to have different feelings toward individuals at different times. Being angry with a class member may be legitimate at times; however, unresolved and lingering anger is unhealthy. Understanding your personal feelings is a significant challenge.

Partners

Teaching opens the door to many partnerships. Each one has the potential for providing a rich, significant experience in teamwork.

A teacher does not teach in a vacuum. Teaching can be viewed as a series of relationships. Let's take a look at some of the possible partnerships available to a teacher—partnership with God, the learner and the class, other teachers and church school leaders, and members of the congregation.

The Teacher and God

Teachers are assured of God's support and interest in teaching activities that tell God's story. Jesus promised to be with us everywhere and always—and that includes teaching. One new teacher said she felt much like a person who was lowered over the side of an ocean liner into a small lifeboat—alone in the vast, dark ocean! And she'd never rowed a boat before in her life! However, be assured that those who teach God's story are not alone.

Regardless of what your faith journey is to date, trust in God. Listen to some voices out of the past. Moses, who didn't want to be a leader, found much strength in the knowledge that God was with him every step of the way. Paul, even in prison, found strength and comfort in God's promises to be at his side. Find confidence in your calling to teach God's story. Cultivate your partnership with God. As you prepare to teach, and then as you are teaching, ask God to be with you each step of the way. Covenant with God to be your partner in teaching.

The Teacher and the Learner

Effective teaching brings every learner into a degree of partnership with the teacher. This can range from the learner who comes to class and sits like a "bump on a log" (children, youth, or adults can do this effectively!) to the learner who is so involved in everything that he or she virtually becomes part of the teaching team. Both types of learners represent partnerships that need to be cultivated and that should never be assumed. Some of the greatest satisfaction you will experience in teaching will come from your relationships with learners. As you increase your partnership with each learner, you will build new bridges of trust. In this way opportunities for learning increase.

The Teacher and the Other Teacher

The best way to begin to teach is in partnership with another teacher. Team teaching is probably the soundest method of teaching because the load of planning, teaching, and evaluating is shared. Another person's insights always add a new dimension to your own thinking. "Two heads are better than one" is a good rule for teachers. When two (or more) teachers work together, the strengths and specialties of each complement the others' and make a teaching team that is more effective than a single individual. You may want to obtain more information about team teaching.

The Teacher and the Class (or Group)

You will create partnerships with individual members of your class. At the same time, you will be creating a relationship with the entire class or group. This partnership will include all the relationships between the group and yourself. There is a difference between one-to-one relationships (the student and you) and group-to-one relationships (all the students and you). There will be times in your thinking and session planning when you will view all students as a group and work toward meeting total class needs, as distinguished from meeting the needs of individual students.

The Teacher and the Church

Christian education is a very important part of a church's total ministry. Leaders in the early Christian church were instructed to teach. Teaching is a gift recognized in the New Testament. The church calls believers to teach the ongoing story of God's work in Jesus Christ. Most churches recognize that each Christian needs to continue to learn and grow in the Christian faith throughout life.

You are acting as a leader of the church when you teach. Many pastors and lay leaders view teaching as one of the most important leadership positions in the local congregation. Regrettably, some church members (and some leaders) do not have the faintest idea about what is happening in their church school.

Remember that your task as teacher is as significant as any other responsibility in your church. You are the potter who molds the clay, both young and old. All minds and lives are pliable, and you touch them in the name of Jesus Christ.

The Teacher and the Board (or Superintendent)

In most churches, large and small, there is a board or committee responsible for the organization and maintenance of the church school. This group recruits teachers and schedules classes. Some boards contact potential teachers personally and obtain a verbal response. Other boards use teaching contracts that clearly spell out their expectations of the teacher.

A wise board or superintendent will pay close attention to the concerns, interests, and needs of the teachers in their school. These people should supply you with a variety of contacts, resources, and encouragement. In larger schools, a departmental superintendent will be your contact person with the board or committee. Whatever the structure, a partnership will be established between you and the organization responsible for the life of your school.

The Teacher and the Pastor

In large churches, few pastors know each teacher personally; in small churches, the pastor knows every teacher by name, what class he or she is teaching, and most of the class members as well. Thus the teacher's relationship with the pastor varies from church to church. What does not vary, however, is the fact that every pastor is a teacher. The sermon is a method of communicating—of teaching. The New Testament clearly states that the leaders of the church (including those whom we today call clergy) have the task of "equipping the saints for ministry." This is an educational task, and it is probably the most important task of the local pastor. The pastor is truly the "teacher of teachers."

Many pastors welcome dialogue with teachers. They are truly interested in what is happening in each class. Pastors need input concerning the needs of congregation members. Do not hesitate to make an appointment with your pastor to share what is happening in your class, to seek advice or guidance, and to develop a mutual concern for your church's ministry of teaching. This is a valuable partnership.

The Teacher and the Parents

Where this partnership applies (classes of children and youth), it affords a great opportunity for the development of meaningful relationships. Church schools need to forge closer ties with parents and the home. Visiting students' homes is as important as careful session preparation. Include parents in your teaching plans. Involve them in your classes or extracurricular activities; communicate with them regularly and build a team relationship with them. Good relationships will pay long-term dividends for the learner, the parents, and yourself.

Note

1. Gabriel Fackre, *The Christian Story* (Grand Rapids, Mich.: Eerdmans, 1978), p. 9.

Chapter 2

Sorting Out the Pieces of the Teaching Puzzle

Beginning teachers often feel as if they are facing an apparently endless maze to which there is no solution. The beginning teacher's experience has been likened to putting together a difficult puzzle. What are all the pieces of the puzzle, and how do they fit together? In this chapter, we take a look at the basic pieces of the puzzle called "teaching."

Teacher Roles

What is expected of a teacher? A teacher who understands what roles he or she is expected to play will be able to function more effectively. The teacher's roles include discipler, communicator, planner, facilitator, creator, translator, and motivator. Let's take a brief look at each of them.

Discipler

The four Gospels show Jesus' teaching efforts focused on challenging those who gathered around him to become his disciples. He rarely taught merely to impart information or content. In each parable, illustration, or story, Jesus clearly tried to persuade those who listened to become his disciples. He wanted them to follow him, to take up their own crosses, and to live out the teachings he gave them.

A disciple is one who subscribes to the teachings of a key teacher

BASIC TEACHER ROLES

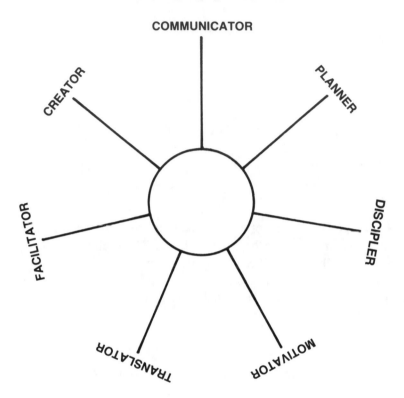

or leader and makes a commitment to promote and spread that person's teachings. You, as a teacher, are a disciple of Jesus Christ. You are a Christian, and by agreeing to teach (and to learn in the process), you are living out the role of a follower of Jesus. You have made a commitment to spread his teachings (through your own teaching). Now think of those who are students in your class. After some sessions (whatever age you teach), you might wonder, Is there any hope? But on other occasions you might conclude, What great potential for disciples!

The members of your class are probably rather ordinary people. As Tom Sine observes, "He didn't call the prominent, affluent community leaders or seminary graduates. He called a collection of terribly ordinary people, many from the unpleasant fringes of Jewish society, some of whom we probably wouldn't want in our churches. He called not only fishermen but tax collectors and political revolutionaries. Unlike the rabbinical schools, Jesus included women among his disciples as well. He also spent a surprising amount of time with children."[1]

It was from this circle of very ordinary people that what we know as Christianity emerged. I think you will agree that, although there are deficiencies and shortcomings in today's churches, Jesus' disciples did their job rather effectively. Each teacher is called not only to *be* a disciple but also to *make* disciples. Each teacher is a *discipler* on behalf of Jesus Christ. What a high calling! What a tremendous opportunity to impact the future of Christ's movement! What a great opportunity to feed, nurture, and encourage your students to become followers of Jesus!

Teachers are communicators. Students are too. Teachers cannot *not* communicate. Neither can students, since teaching generates a constant flow of communication. Teachers teach through both words and actions (verbal and nonverbal communication). Sometimes our actions speak louder than our words. Effective communication is a two-way street. Every student needs (and most students thrive on) two-way communication. Study the first steps of a communication circle in the diagram that follows. These first communication steps are used by *all* teachers.

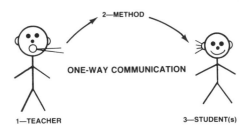

Explanation

1. The teacher prepares a message to be sent to a receiver (the student). This could be a session plan, a Bible story, a song, a

thought, an expression of caring, a joke, a hope, an admonition, and so on.

2. The teacher selects the best method by which to send the message after considering *all* the possibilities. Some possibilities might be a story, a drama, a lecture, a song, a reading from the Bible, a visit, the VCR, the TV—among many others.

3. The student receives the message. At this moment, the student attempts to unravel the message sent by the teacher. Success depends on the message's being clear and important to the student, more so than to the teacher!

Look at the diagram again. Does the teacher *know* whether the student has received the message he or she sent? Was the method selected the *right* one? How can the teacher find out if communication *really took place?*

Many things can go wrong when a message is received (by a teacher or a student). Sometimes the students receive messages that were never intentionally transmitted, and messages can get sent that the teacher did not intend to send. For these and other reasons, teachers can never be sure if communication has taken place at this point. At step 3, the teacher does not know if he or she has communicated.

Now the teacher needs to encourage the student to become the sender of a return message. Let's look at the rest of the communication circle.

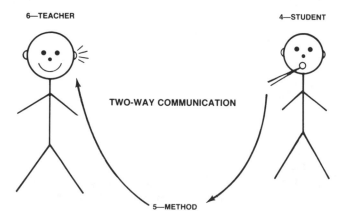

4. The student is encouraged to become a sender of a message back to the teacher or class.

5. The new sender now must select a method of communicating with the first sender (the teacher). Possible communication methods range from claps of happiness, applause, laughter, affirmative head nodding, eye contact, singing, another question, wonderment—or blank stares, a yawn, or an absence next Sunday.

6. The teacher now becomes the receiver. What message did the students send you in response to the message you sent them? Was it what you expected? If not, what went wrong? What needs to be changed? Are you challenged by the message you received? (Note: At first glance, this illustration of two-way communication may appear to refer only to a lecture style of teaching. However, every method of communication, whether as brief as a word, a look, or a touch, or as long as a half-hour lecture, holds the possibility for two-way communication. The teacher should look for and provide opportunities for two-way communication to take place whatever the circumstances or method of teaching.)

Some teachers do not complete this circle of communication for a variety of reasons, including: I don't want to receive it because it might be threatening, distasteful, or hurtful; I don't have time to receive it; it's not important to me now; I didn't really expect them to understand it anyway.

Steps 4 through 6 do not always need to immediately follow steps 1 through 3. A full session plan can be a message to the students. A unit of sessions can also be a message. It is best to have some evaluation, no matter how brief, after each session. Otherwise you run the risk of teaching session after session with no message being received.

Some messages need to be checked out immediately. Communication about what is being sent or received needs to happen at that moment.

Please note that true communication does *not* take place until the message has been sent to the receiver and returned, in whatever form, to the sender. Only in this way can the teacher know if the message sent (caring, sharing, story, love, truth, for example) was actually received by the student.

There is a fine line between communicating and manipulating. When you send your message, is the receiver completely free to respond with whatever message he or she wishes to return to you? Or must the receiver send back only the message you want to hear? If your objective is for the students to respond like puppets on a string, then you will (and can) manipulate. However, if you believe that students learn by having the freedom to "tell it like it is," you will be a communicator.

The importance of completing the circle of communication cannot be overstated. Thousands of students have dropped out of church schools over the past decade without any attempt ever being made to discover what was really being communicated, either by them or by the schools. What actually happened was that communication did not take place—and the message to the school and the teacher was, I don't want it, or like it, or need it, or believe it. The future demands effective and honest communication, and the only way this can happen is to establish a two-way system of communication.

To conclude, this is what two-way communication looks like when all the steps have been included:

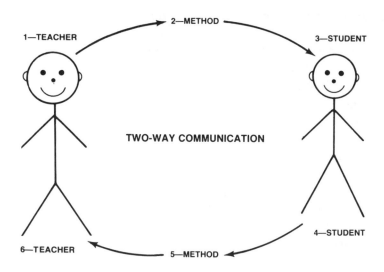

Planner

Every teacher is a planner. The question is, What kind? Unless you approach your class without ever having looked at the material, you have done at least some planning. There are different ways for teachers to plan, just as there are different ways to prepare sermons (and you can usually tell the difference!). There are, unfortunately, many ineffective planning styles. Some teachers spend their time planning (often not enough) on late Saturday night or early Sunday morning. Some try to plan the lesson in front of the TV, but find that time spent in planning directly corresponds to the length of commercials. Another well-intentioned but mostly ineffective style is to write notes on scraps of paper during the week; the plan fails when the notes are lost or left at home. Some teachers start out well by beginning to plan on Sunday afternoon for the following week, but they may never get back to it until late Saturday night.

The description could go on, but the important thing to remember is that planning a session takes time. Read it again—*planning takes time*. Each teacher needs to be creative, and creativity takes time. Each teacher needs to be an effective communicator, and good communication takes time. Each teacher needs to pray, and prayer takes time. And so it takes time to plan a session. As you gain more experience with teaching, you will be able to put together a session plan more quickly. However, if you wish to be a creative, effective, and interesting teacher, you will need to invest some time. Over the years, desperate church education leaders have recruited teachers by telling them that it's easy, there's nothing to it, and it won't take that much time. But on the contrary, it does take time, and it is not easy. For this reason it amounts to hard work in today's busy world. But experienced teachers know that the hard work required to make teaching meaningful is rewarded as they see learners of all ages grow in faith and Christian living.

One of the main reasons for the large number of students dropping out of church schools during the past decade has been the unwillingness or the inability of many teachers to offer interesting, original, creative, and meaningful classes. The net result has been boredom—and dropouts. Additional time spent in preparation and in gaining an understanding of the task will usually provide a much better teaching/learning experience. It doesn't take a lot of time to be a "phony" (Saturday night planner), but it does take time to be a "real" teacher.

The best way to plan each week's session is to begin early in the week. Better yet, try to work several weeks ahead, if your schedule permits. Try to find a regular time each week when you can do your basic planning. Later in the week, some of the details can be added. If you are a member of a teaching team, your planning schedule will have to coincide with the others'. It may take several months to discover the best way to do your planning.

A key to being a good planner is to work at being organized. Jim and Mary taught a middler class (grades 3-4). Midway through a session, an excellent opportunity arose for the group to work on a collage. Although not part of their session plan, the collage was one of the backup possibilities they had identified. They would have to eliminate something else if it was used. Out came their box of supplies, which included material for backup as well as planned activities. They found the items needed and proceeded with the activity. They not only prepared well but also had a backup plan and brought materials for both the basic session plan and the backup plan.

In another classroom Ted and Sue were team teaching a senior high class. They too had an opportunity to use a supplementary activity, one that called for turnover charts. In fact, they had discussed this extra option as they made their plans, but they decided there probably wouldn't be time for it. As a result, they didn't have the charts with them, and the opportunity was lost.

Jim and Mary were well organized—they had thoroughly prepared for all possibilities, had organized their thinking and resources, and were flexible when the moment of readiness arrived. Although Ted and Sue had planned, they had not organized for all the possibilities. The result was a missed opportunity for their group to use the "right method at the right moment." Teachers who are not well organized can teach, but the task is facilitated by good organization.

What needs to be organized? Most of the teaching elements listed here can be improved with better organization by the teacher:

- approach to the session
- the classroom
- communication before and after sessions
- agreements and understandings with students
- awareness of calendars, dates, deadlines, etc.
- session planning
- follow-up strategies
- evaluation and feedback
- available resources
- personal growth

Facilitator

A facilitator is a person who makes something easier for someone else. If the word is new to you, try to become familiar with its meaning because it is a key word for teaching in today's church school. A teacher cannot "make" students learn, any more than a teacher can "make" them show up every Sunday. But a concerned teacher can facilitate learning as well as attendance. A dedicated teacher will do everything in his or her power to make learning easier, more delightful, and truly attractive.

When a child is old enough to learn to tie shoelaces, a parent may or may not facilitate this learning experience for the child. On one extreme, a parent can continue to tie the child's laces forever—or until one or the other feels embarrassed by it. A facilitating parent will use many different ways to assist the child in learning. Some ways to facilitate this learning would be to explain the process carefully, show the child how to do it, guide his or her hands in the tying process, laugh together when the bows don't turn out right and form hard knots, and celebrate successes. Helping to make something easy calls for patience, observation, listening, and encouragement. There is a big difference between the teacher who "does everything" for the group and the teacher who is an effective facilitator so that real learning can take place. The most effective learning takes place when the learners are actively involved by teachers.

Creator

Teaching in today's world requires creativity, something not clearly recognized in years past. Since God's story is about new life, it is appropriate for the teacher to be a creator with his or her class. Creativity is, for most of us, a capacity that needs to be developed. The creative teacher is ever alert to new possibilities for presenting the session, keeping old relationships fresh, and developing new relationships.

In order to be creative, a teacher must be able to see potential for change in the class, in the lives of students, and in the content being presented. Creativity involves risk—the risk of having something "fall flat on its face." However, continually striving for creativity will eventually tell you what you can expect from yourself and the class.

Why be creative? God is our Creator—we are the people of God. The story of creation itself unfolds with almost unbelievable creativity. As the people of God, we have the task of reflecting God, who is not old and stale but is alive and well. God is not like a stagnant pool, but a fresh, moving stream—ever new. We have not even begun to measure God's depths. However, creative teachers can begin to discover and help others to discover new glimpses and visions of a God who is ever new. Attempt to create new images, relationships, meanings, and experiences for yourself and your students, with God and with each other.

Translator

A translator carries a message from one person or cultural context to another. One of the teacher's roles is that of translator. The Bible's story needs to be translated into the lives of your students. An effective translator needs to be familiar with the language, culture, frames of reference, and background of both parties—in this case, God's story and your students. All teachers of the story need an ever increasing awareness and understanding of the Scriptures. Knowledge of Scripture will help you present Jesus Christ as a real person—someone to get excited about and someone to commit your life to. The teacher needs not only a working knowledge of the Bible but also familiarity with the world of the student. Where does each student (young or old) spend most of her time? What does his world look like? Is it like your world? Is it different? If so, what makes it different? As a teacher, you need to know the background, home life, school or work context, personalities, and character traits (as much as you possibly can) of your students in order to understand their world better. It is into their world that you will be translating God's story. To illustrate, we know that contemporary music is one of the main components of contemporary culture. How can you, the teacher, use the medium of music to assist you in translating God's story into the lives of today's teens?

If you teach children, it is important to know when and how to use the familiar terms "father" and "mother." The increasing number of broken homes today is producing an increasing number of children with very different perceptions of what these terms mean. You need to be aware of each child's background in order to be a successful translator of terms that imply parental love, care, and concern. Teachers need to be good listeners and observers in order to be effective translators.

Motivator

Another role of the teacher is to motivate persons to meet God through Jesus Christ, learn about God's teachings, and allow this relationship to affect everything he or she does. Every student needs to be motivated and encouraged to learn. In the springtime, the sun encourages seeds to emerge from the ground into new life. They grow up to flower and bear fruit of their own kind. Similarly, the role of the teacher is to encourage each student to grow and blossom, to create a climate for growth, to provide warmth and encouragement to grow, and to affirm the growth that takes place in each student. Indeed, teachers are motivators. This is particularly true in a church school that students are not compelled to attend. As time goes by, you will discover which students need more motivation and which have a degree of self-motivation.

There are many ways to develop your ability to motivate people. The teaching roles described in this chapter call for the teacher to motivate. As you learn to increase your effectiveness as a teacher, you will increase your ability to motivate. For instance, students who have nothing to say about decisions that affect their class are apt to show little interest or concern. They just drift along, content to let time pass. However, participation generates enthusiasm. Discover ways to involve the members of your class in the teaching/learning process. This includes preparation, in-class activities, translating the session into life, and evaluating what happened. Involve students in the life of your class to the fullest extent possible. In most cases, this will increase their motivation to learn.

In summary, basic teacher roles described in this chapter include the following:

Discipler	Communicator	Planner	Facilitator
Creator	Translator	Motivator	

Right about now, you may be feeling overwhelmed by all that has been presented. You may be feeling that there is no way you can fulfill all these roles. But the truth is that not even those of us who have taught for years are able to fulfill all of these roles with maximum effectiveness all of the time. Rather than attempting to do that, each teacher needs to assess where he or she is in relationship to each role and then decide where to begin to improve teacher efficiency in several of the areas.

Consider each role and then estimate your degree of awareness and efficiency in regard to it on the form provided on the next page. Remember, this is just a place to begin. As time goes by, you will (without being aware of it) develop skills and abilities that will improve your effectiveness in many of the areas.

The Biggest Pieces in the Puzzle

We've talked about the teacher and the student, but there are other pieces in the teaching puzzle. Some pieces are much bigger than the others and need to be put together before the rest of the puzzle can be completed. Jan Chartier, well-known Christian educator, teacher, and trainer, after years of analyzing Christian education philosophy and methodology, has identified three pieces that she considers keys to the teaching puzzle: the teacher, the student,

Basic Teacher Role	Very Effective	Somewhat Effective	Not too Effective	Not Effective at All
1. Discipler				
2. Communicator				
3. Planner				
4. Facilitator				
5. Creator				
6. Translator				
7. Motivator				

and the content. The diagram on the next page shows how they interact.

You are already familiar with teacher and student roles. By content we mean everything dealt with by the teacher and the student in an educational experience. Some of the content "ingredients" include printed curriculum, the Bible, teaching methods, teaching resources (audiovisuals, cassettes, videotapes, etc.), the classroom experience, the community(ies) in which church, teacher, and students are located, the needs of students, feelings (student's and teacher's), relationships, as well as what happened yesterday and last week.

The arrows indicate movement in all directions. The bracket brings the teacher and learner together and indicates that at times they move toward or respond to content as one.

The diagram shows all channels open—movement is possible in every direction. However, for a variety of reasons, channels can be blocked or closed. One of the teacher's tasks is to attempt to open channels that become blocked, regardless of the reason. The flow between the student and the content can be blocked for some time

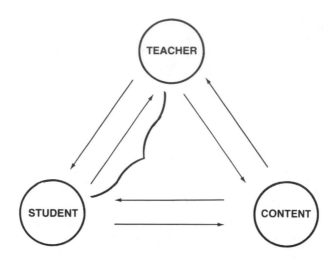

before a teacher becomes aware of the problem. Regular evaluation, coupled with good listening and observation, is important to keeping all channels open.

The issue in teaching is learning. All that a teacher does in preparation to teach is directed toward student learning. Learning is gaining knowledge and understanding of the content in such a way that all of life is affected. To attempt to teach without learning taking place is an exercise in futility and a waste of everyone's time. The task of the teacher is to bring the student and the content together. Bridges of all types should be built between the content and the student in order for the best learning to take place.

Learning takes place in different ways. Each student learns in a variety of ways. Here are some different ways of learning:

- learning by doing
- learning by listening
- learning by repetition
- learning by threat
- learning by reading
- learning by observing
- learning by idolizing
- learning by forgetting
- learning by accident
- learning by caring

- learning by watching a demonstration
- learning by memorizing
- learning by behavior
- learning by making mistakes
- learning by being corrected
- learning by being punished
- learning by sharing
- learning through suffering
- learning by exaggeration

- learning by experimentation   • learning by teaching
- learning by failing

Which ways of learning do you feel are most useful? Which of them have been most helpful to you? Place a check mark ($\checkmark$) to the left of each item through which you have learned. Place an X to the right of each item you feel is a valid way to learn. Circle each way to learn that you would eventually like to use in your teaching. Place a star (*) by your favorite way to learn. You can learn a lot about your students by sharing this list with them and learning what they like.

Professor Edgar Dale has organized the variety of ways that learning takes place into a pyramid according to degree of effectiveness. The ones included near the top of the pyramid are considered to be least effective, while those at the bottom provide greater effectiveness. As you teach, you will choose a variety of methods and will want to use the ones that provide the greatest opportunity for learning to take place.

Consider this statement by Norman De Puy, pastor, speaker, and church leader:

> For two hundred years we in the Protestant church have built "attendance badge empires" of people who know about the facts of the Bible, complete with the numbers of the verses (just as if they were important) but who know little personally, in their hearts, of the radical love of God, a love that would challenge selfishness, racism, all sorts of isms that compete with the holy righteousness of the living God who demands to be first, last and all in all.
>
> A physical knowledge of the Bible is good, but not nearly so important for the child as you might think. Because a child can recite the books of the Bible, or because he can find his place quickly in a "sword drill" can be worse than nothing if it causes the child to think that because he can do these tricks he knows the Bible.

De Puy raises a question that is significant to teachers and churches: How do persons learn? Do students learn by being given facts and then repeating them? Do students learn when the teacher chooses the simplest form of curriculum that can be found, waits until Saturday night to prepare, and fully expects God to bless this effort? Is a quick answer to a question the best way to teach, or is it more effective to work with students to seek answers even if the searching takes time?

A number of years ago at Camp Judson near Erie, Pennsylvania, certain campers were screaming and carrying on near the deep end of the camp pond. It was free time, and sixteen or seventeen campers were crowded together in a rather small circle precariously near the edge of the pond. Running to the pond, I observed them jumping around, pushing each other in and out of the circle, and I imagined the worst. Several counselors came running too. Working our way into the group, we soon discovered that the center of attraction was a snake, neatly coiled in the grass, its tongue darting rapidly in and out. The snake was about three feet long and had a thick body with brightly colored markings on it. Since it was surrounded by frenzied campers, the safest thing for it to do was to stay put.

The big question was, What kind of snake is it? It was identified as everything from an extra large garter snake to a boa constrictor. Many were sure that it was a rattlesnake; others thought it was a water moccasin, and so it went. Upon our arrival, the group immediately wanted us to clear up the mystery by telling them what kind of snake it was. However, instead of answering their question directly, we asked the group to sit down on the ground around the snake and talk about what we saw. While doing this, we asked them how they could find out what kind of snake it was on their own. One of them suddenly remembered the camp library, and off they went for books. Several books on reptiles were brought back. The campers gathered in small clusters to thumb through the pages, all the while keeping an eye on the snake. For some unknown reason, the snake made no effort to get away.

Soon they found their answer. It was a good-sized water snake— harmless. The counselors could have told them that when they arrived. But the campers were able to find their own answer to their own question! What could have been resolved in a moment became a learning experience that lasted an hour. And it wasn't over yet!

That night, counselors and other campers listened to the exciting

DALE'S CONE OF LEARNING [2]

Dale's cone is based on the simple formula that persons remember only 10 percent of what they hear, 50 percent of what they see and hear, and 90 percent of what they do.

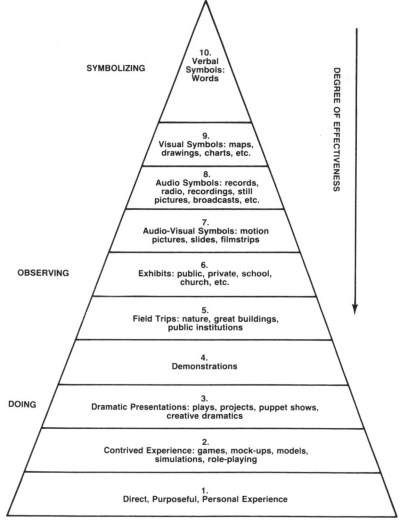

[2] Adapted from Edgar Dale, *Audio-Visual Methods in Teaching*, rev. ed. (New York: Holt, Rinehart & Winston, 1954), chapter 4.

story about the snake. In fact, you were a very important person in the eyes of other campers if you had been there! As the stories wore on, questions began to be raised about the "why" of snakes. Why did God create snakes? What if one of them had been bitten—what would the others have done? If the snake had attacked one of them (quite a fantasy!), would someone else have given his or her life for that person? The door was opened to talk about Jesus, and the conversation became profound. In this setting counselors and campers were able to share their feelings, fears, beliefs, and dreams about something real that had happened to all of them that day. The experience also eventually turned all of their minds toward God. But it is important to note that the counselors could have "killed" the whole experience by giving a quick answer that afternoon. Fortunately, they refused to give one-word answers and chose to teach by sharing and caring.

A simplified version of Dale's Cone of Learning would look like this:

WORDS	Ear-gate
SEEING	Eye-gate
PRETENDING/SIMULATING	Acting it out
REAL LIFE EXPERIENCES	Living it out

You have probably observed more than once that people don't always *hear* what you say. Perhaps some of them just don't pay attention, and some may not want to hear what you're saying. And there will be some people who don't *understand* what you say. Whether conversing casually or speaking in a classroom setting, you assume that people will hear, pay attention, and respond. But most of us are rather passive when it comes to the ear-gate—we can take it or leave it. If what we hear is new, loud, or exciting, we may listen. If it isn't, we may not listen. For example, how long would you leave the TV turned on if there were no picture? Enough said!

Seeing adds another dimension. Pictures, objects, media, and other visual aids provide many more possibilities for learners to respond than words alone. It is easier to turn off words than visuals. Of course, words and visuals are most effective when used together.

Acting or pretending (simulating) adds a significant dimension to learning activities. Examples of this method include role-playing, drama, creative writing, debating, certain kinds of field trips, simulation games, and other similar types of activities. In a safe setting under Christian guidance learners can pretend to deal with issues, challenges, opportunities, or problems. Although the activities are not real, they are usually stimulating enough to help learners gain insights into themselves, Scripture, and other people.

I often tell church leaders that the best learning situations occur outside the classroom in the so-called real world. Unfortunately most of the church's learning experiences are offered inside the church building. Of course it *is* quite possible to have some real-life experiences in church, but it doesn't happen very often. For instance, I have worked with teachers and leaders to provide opportunities for children's classes to teach adult classes once a quarter. The same can be done with youth classes. The reverse can also be true. A great learning experience for an adult class or group is to plan a session with children or youth. It is a revelation to the average adult to wrestle with what concerns today's children and youth. The adults probably learn more than the children or youth. Yet another stimulating experience is to have a young adult class prepare a session for an older adult group or class. After a month or two, reverse the teaching roles of the classes.

There are unlimited opportunities outside the church for real-life learning experiences. For example, consider the Scripture in which Jesus suggested we give a cup of cold water in his name. Live it out some hot summer Sunday morning or afternoon (or other day). Visiting hospitals, nursing homes, or other church members creates all kinds of real-life possibilities for the Good News to come alive.

Sharing and Caring—The Heart of Teaching

Sharing and caring are essential to learning. The task of the teacher is to share God's story and one's self. Sharing *without* caring for the students as persons makes teaching much less effective. In fact, the teacher who gives little evidence of caring for his or her students can turn them away from the gospel, since the teacher (a Christian) can be seen as hypocritical. On the other hand, caring for students without sharing God's story defeats the very purpose of

Christian teaching. In the following diagram, the teacher is shown to have equal opportunities for sharing and caring. The acts of sharing and caring are directed at each student and at the class as a whole. It is the teacher's hope that the student will respond to both the sharing and the caring and that some of the response will be directed toward the class itself. Sharing content within the class and experiencing meaningful relationships are important objectives. The teacher can also hope that each student will, upon leaving the classroom experience, become a sharing, caring person in all of life's settings.

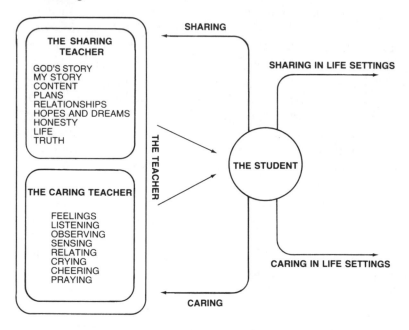

There is little need for teachers who are experts, who "know all the answers" and give them to their students. The need is for teachers who can be friendly and are willing to share with and care for each student. The typical classroom setting tends to bring the student and the content together in isolation from life itself. The teacher and student need to escape this isolation by discovering sharing and caring in the classroom whenever possible and transporting it into the everyday life of both students and teacher.

Learning Is Using

Successful teaching implies the ability to import knowledge or understanding (of content, relationships, feelings, etc.) into the life of another person in such a way that it has some practical value. De Puy says:

Knowing about Moses and the bulrushes is not going to do a bit of good unless you understand in your gut that Moses was a stuttering, incompetent murderer who was used by God because that is the kind of God he is. He is the kind of God that loves little kids, and all sorts of people who don't yet know who they are for sure, and the meaning of the bulrushes; the love of God for all of us needs to be experienced. Learning facts by themselves isn't going to make kids experience that love.

When the session has been translated and absorbed into the life of the student in a usable form, learning has taken place. Successful student learning is "student using." "Using" may be short- or long-range. Every session should focus on the needs that students experience in their everyday lives.

Learning is conditioned by expectations. This includes the expectations of the teacher, the student, the church, and sometimes parent or spouse. Most teachers expect something to happen when they are teaching. What do you expect to happen? Your expectations will emerge from session planning, God's story, and the student. Teacher expectations provide direction for the teaching/learning experience. However, they need to be joined with the student's expectations. Sometimes expectations are changed by outside factors such as the classroom, current events, etc. If you must teach in a place where you and your class have no protection from the noise and movement of other groups, your expectations, as well as those of the students, may need to be revised.

Learning Is "Togetherness" Teaching

Over the years, there have been many approaches to teaching. For a variety of reasons, most of them have ignored the principle of "togetherness." It is one thing to be together in a classroom where the teacher teaches and the students learn. It is another style of teaching altogether when teacher and students move out of the classroom into real-life settings where students and teacher become a teaching team. In Dale's Cone of Learning, the most effective level of learning is the bottom line—"direct, purposeful, personal experience." Togetherness teaching takes the student out of the classroom *with the teacher* into situations where student and teacher can teach and work together. In the simplified version of the Cone of Learning, this is living-it-out-in-the-real-world kind of teaching/learning. It is universally accepted in the world of sports, for instance, that a team and its coach belong together. Have you ever seen a game in which the team played without the coach's presence to guide, direct, exhort, encourage, and challenge? When baseball teams play, whether Little League or major league, the coaches are always present. This is the rule for every sport.

Over the years, our church schools have assumed that in an hour or less on Sunday, teachers could give a student enough content, motivation, interpretation, and inspiration to equip that person to live God's story in everyday life. Laity and clergy view Christian education in our churches as a system of "schooling." This is far from the truth. Biblically speaking, Christian education is about life—about learning a way of life. The Bible is about people, feelings, relationships, and commitment. To treat the Bible as no more than a book of facts does an injustice to the Word of God. The Bible is a book about life; and for maximum learning to take place, real life is the best context in which to teach. Remember that Jesus did little teaching in a classroom. Rather, he used every life setting and experience he came upon as his teaching context.

It is difficult to translate God's story into real life in the classroom. Somehow, some of the learning experiences need an added dimension of life itself. Currently, the coach (teacher) teaches them on Sunday, and the players (students) are sent out on Monday to play the game alone, with no coach and no other team members! Rather than separating the players (students) from the coaches (teachers) as the church school has done, we need to bring them together in real-life situations. This principle is illustrated in an anecdote that comes from the First Baptist Church of Downey, California.

As a church member mowed his grass one day, two carloads of middle-school students (grades 6-8) from the church passed by. They honked and shouted in typically enthusiastic fashion. They were calling on their friends. Betty Neilan, the church minister to middlers, and her intern assistant, John McNabb, had an outreach program for a number of kids to do visitation of their friends. They made thirty-seven calls!

The kind of staff *motivation and teaching* illustrated in this anecdote is exactly what our faith and our church are all about. Missionary zeal, evangelistic purpose, and the fulfillment of the Great Commission ("Go ye") are happening here.

A great deal of learning about life and the Bible can take place when students (young and old) and teachers are together in real-life situations. Real life includes not only doing "church things" but also having social times together, doing work or service projects, or, sometimes, just being together. It is impossible to teach the game of baseball by telling someone about it in a classroom. It is impossible to learn how to play hockey in a classroom, even if the teacher is a coach. You need a baseball field for one and a skating rink or pond for the other—then real learning begins.

Jesus set the example for this kind of teaching. He and the disciples had many conversations about the kingdom. He described it in a variety of ways, and they asked many questions. Finally he told them to take up their cross and follow him (Matthew 16:24). Now they would find out what the kingdom was about. Teacher and students would be together in whatever was ahead. They had talked about it long enough. Now—together—crosses. After sharing experiences, they would gather and talk about what had happened. This was teaching at its best.

Too many students, both young and old, are capable of repeating words, concepts, and phrases. But that's all they know. The message is in their heads but not in their lives. Until they actually experience the words, concepts, and phrases, God's story has not been translated effectively.

How can a teacher accomplish togetherness teaching? It isn't easy. It requires time, which often works against the volunteer teacher. What is referred to as an "hour" of teaching on Sunday

morning rarely adds up to sixty minutes; in many church schools it
is no more than forty to forty-five minutes, which is not enough
time to do this kind of teaching. On a deeper level, however, the
issue is not as much a matter of time as it is of location. As long as
God's story continues to be taught within four walls, having no
context other than the class itself, the task is next to impossible. The
church school must free its students and teachers—together! There
are many benefits of togetherness teaching, a few of which are listed
here.

1. Teacher and students work on a common objective outside the
classroom.

2. A variety of new and different settings for learning and service
are discovered outside the classroom.

3. New and different ways to share God's story will be identified.

4. There are many different ways to care for each other and for
persons outside the class.

5. The Bible can come alive, instead of being just a book of facts.

6. Students and teachers make decisions together.

7. Students and teachers learn how to plan together.

8. These experiences can supplement the unit of sessions being
taught.

9. Students become teachers and leaders in real-life settings.

10. A class can learn to give itself away. (See Matthew 16:25-26.)

11. Facts, content, and stories can be translated into real life.

12. Witness possibilities exist in real-life settings.

13. Learning increases when you reflect together on what you
have done.

I am not suggesting that you leave the classroom every Sunday.
However, with the exception of the nursery and the aged, almost
every class will profit from moving into a "life setting" from time
to time. Just one such life-setting experience with the teacher every
few months can provide "grist for the mill" for many sessions.
Scheduling possibilities for this activity include once a month, once
a unit, or once in a six-month period of teaching.

Now consider some suggestions for togetherness teaching. As
time goes by, you will think of many others.

1. Every class should have at least one relationship with a

person(s) or family with whom they can minister. For instance, a class could be involved in the life of an elderly person in meaningful ways. Any class of any age level can provide Bible study, prayer, singing, and Christian fellowship to elderly Christians who can no longer attend church. Students can be teachers when the class shares with the elderly. The possibilities are unlimited for ministry throughout the year.

A teacher wrote recently about a visit that her young students (grades 1-3) paid to the oldest member of their congregation on a Sunday afternoon. They planned to visit for a few minutes and sing one song.

However, the visit lasted over half an hour and included many songs and much conversation. The children and the ninety-three-year-old shut-in had a thoroughly enjoyable time. Said the teacher, "I was amazed at the rapport between a senior member and eight little noisy boys and one little girl."

Persons who work in nursing homes tell me that the lonely residents eagerly anticipate special events involving children or animals. Ministry to the elderly is an important challenge to which the church school can respond. Matthew 25:35-40 says, "'For I was hungry and you gave me food, I was thirsty and you gave me something to drink, I was a stranger and you welcomed me, I was naked and you gave me clothing, I was sick and you took care of me, I was in prison and you visited me.' Then the righteous will answer him, 'Lord, when was it that we saw you hungry and gave you food, or thirsty and give you something to drink? And when was it that we saw you a stranger and welcomed you, or naked and gave you clothing? And when was it that we say you sick or in prison and visited you?' And the king will answer them, 'Truly, I tell you, just as you did it to one of the least of these who are members of my family, you did it to me.'"

2. Many institutionalized persons have no relatives or friends who visit or care. They need to get away from their place of residence (nursing home, for example), but have no place to go. Some nursing homes are willing to permit some residents to go out for a meal in a private home, a party, or just a friendly evening gathering. A class of teens could plan a meal in one of their homes

or in the church for a guest from a nursing home. Some could
provide transportation; others could prepare a meal, while others
could work on a brief fellowship time.

3. A class and its teacher can do more than talk about witnessing—they can *be* witnesses. To talk forever about the need to
witness to our faith but never do it together as students and teachers
provides little opportunity for learning to take place.

4. If time is crucial and no other time can be found, use the
Sunday morning class time. What greater way for a class to discover
what its community is like than to visit the community on Sunday
morning? Obviously, this doesn't need to be done every Sunday;
but if it happens with some degree of frequency, it will provide
many contexts for learning that can never be produced in the
classroom.

At a weekend lab for youth and youth ministers that was held in
a western Pennsylvania community, it was decided that during the
church school hour participants would knock on doors in the
community. Students were interested in learning what people did
on Sunday morning when they didn't go to church. Teachers and
other adults accompanied each group as observers. Youth were to
ring doorbells, speak with those who answered, and carry on the
dialogue. If the occasion arose, they were to tell about their local
church.

Each group of students had much to talk about when it returned.
One group, in particular, had a most unusual story. The students
began with the house that was next door to the church. When they
knocked on the door of an apartment, there was no response. As
they started to leave, they heard some movement inside. The door
opened, and there was a fairly young man in a wheelchair. They
shared what they were doing, and he invited them in. They
discovered that he was a Christian who had been unable to attend
church for over five years. Most of all, he yearned for a Communion service and asked if they could hold one right there in
his home. A hasty huddle raised some questions about grape juice
and bread. It was decided that they could use bread and water because
he had no grape juice. So in his small living room, youth and adults
sat on the floor around him and shared the most meaningful

Communion experience of their lives. They served each other with trembling hands and prayed.

Imagine! This took place right next door to the church. And it only happened because this class was freed to leave the classroom to experience life itself. The gospel of Jesus Christ is about life. The Bible is a book about life. Let's unlock the doors of our church schools to life!

5. A class can experience "giving itself away." What happens when a class gives itself away? The illustrations we have considered describe classes and groups that gave themselves away. There is much evidence in Scripture that giving is at the heart of Christianity. From the Christmas story to the cross, Christianity is about giving.

6. Interaction between classes is another way to create different learning experiences. Bring together a class of middle-school students with a class of middle-aged adults, and you provide two new sets of relationships for both. Each group could prepare a lesson for the other. Classes could share projects or programs. It would be good for middle-aged adults to hear the Christmas story told by primary children while visiting in the primary classroom. And it would be a good learning experience for an adult class to teach the junior class at Easter. To interpret the resurrection story for juniors would be a challenge for adults.

7. Sometimes projects can help a class come to grips with the reality of life and God's story. They also serve to free the class from the classroom, depending on the nature of the project. A class could help someone else by insulating the home of an elderly person, a handicapped person, or a poor family. Giving a garden away is a great opportunity to learn what work, sharing, and caring is about.

These are but a few ideas of what togetherness teaching is about. Its purpose is to lead teacher and students out of the classroom to share and care in real life *together.* Students need to have experiences like these with their teacher, just as ballplayers need to have their coaches with them when they play a game. To train (teach) the players (students) and then leave them when the game begins isn't the best way for learning to take place.

You, the teacher, are the key to togetherness teaching. You must be "sold" on the idea for it to succeed. Jeanette Perkins Brown has emphasized the importance of the teacher: "Rarely does anything of lasting value happen in the classroom the possibility of which has not first passed through the mind of the teacher." You can sow these kinds of seeds. Not every class will be ready—or willing—to pursue learning this way. Sow your seeds after you have carefully prepared the soil. The most opportune time cannot be predicted, but you will sense the moment when your class may be ready. When you are ready to attempt to introduce togetherness teaching to your class, begin with a small, manageable idea or plan. Don't begin with a project so big or imposing that success may be difficult to achieve. Begin small and then build. Free your class, at the appropriate time, to experience God's story in real life *with you as their guide.*

Notes

1. Tom Sine, *Taking Discipleship Seriously* (Valley Forge, Pa.: Judson, 1985), p. 22.

2. Adapted from Edgar Dale, *Audio-Visual Methods in Teaching,* rev. ed. (New York: Holt, Rinehart and Winston, 1954), chap. 4.

3. Glee Yoder, "Happiness Is . . . a Church School Teacher," *Baptist Leader* 41, no. 10 (January 1980): 7.

Chapter 3

The Teacher's Dozen: Planning a Session in Thirteen Steps

The best way to study this chapter is to read through it once without looking at printed curriculum materials. Then read through the chapter again, this time referring to your materials. (If you are not yet teaching, ask for a set of teacher/student materials for the age level you would like to teach in your church school.)

Photocopy the cutout labels found on the next page and use them to identify the parts of a session plan as you put it together. These labels will serve as a checklist for you. If you are a member of a teaching team, you may be working with teachers who do not feel the need to label the planning steps. However, you are encouraged to use them even when you plan with the other members of your teaching team. Here are some "rules" to consider for planning a session.

One of the first rules in session planning is to write everything out on paper—and then keep the paper. The mind is a great container, but it can hold only so much. Weeks after you have taught a session, you may want to refer to the plan you used, and the best way to be sure it's there is to have it in writing.

A second rule is to plan in sequence. Some things should happen before others. When you are baking a cake, certain steps come before others. Automobiles aren't produced by first filling the gas tank. Before you design your closing activity, you need to determine

THE TEACHER'S DOZEN

PRAYER 1	READING 2	LAST WEEK 3
CONCERNS 4	UNIT GOAL(S) 5	LEARNING OBJECTIVES 6
SESSION OUTLINE 7	OPENING ACTIVITIES 8	TEACHING ACTIVITIES 9
CLOSING ACTIVITIES 10	PARTICIPATION 11	MATERIALS, RESOURCES 12
	EVALUATION 13	

everything that will happen prior to the conclusion of the session. Use the numbered labels to help you keep everything in the right sequence.

Another rule to remember is that all the parts of your session plan must be related in some way, including last week's session and next week's session. The careful planner will see that the overarching unit goal connects one week to another, tying all your sessions together. The same is true about the parts of each individual session plan. The beginning and the ending should be related. The objectives, the teaching activities, student participation, and so forth, should also be related.

Step 1: Prayer

Begin by asking God's help in planning and teaching the session. Remember the partnership between God and the teacher that we identified in chapter 1. Now is the time to claim that promise of support, strength, and understanding—the very presence of God that Scripture tells us is available: "When they call to me, I will answer them; I will be with them in trouble, I will rescue them and honor them" (Psalm 91:15). "Ask, and it will be given you; search, and you will find; knock, and the door will be opened to you. For everyone who asks receives, and everyone who searches finds, and for everyone who knocks, the door will be opened" (Matthew 7:7-8). Other helpful verses include Romans 8:26; 1 Thessalonians 5:17; 1 John 3:22. Keep the label in front of you while you plan as a reminder of this very important step.

Step 2: Reading

Read and study the printed material. There are two reading steps that need to be emphasized. Use the reading label to remind you to do this step.

1. Read the unit. When you receive your printed curriculum, it will usually cover a period of three months, or a *quarter.* Do a complete reading of the quarterly material. One teacher reads through her curriculum resources as soon as she receives them, making notes of ideas that come to mind. Then she meets with other members of the teaching team who have done the same thing. Together they develop quarterly goals and objectives, after which they work on individual sessions. This preliminary step is much like buying a home. When you view the house or apartment for the first time, you see the "big picture." You observe the most outstanding features about the house as well as the setting, the trees and shrubs, the neighboring residences. You try to visualize your life in this setting. All this happens before you see a closet, the bathroom, or the basement. Or this preliminary step can be likened to buying a car. First you inspect the whole car from top to bottom and from front to back. You already have some feelings and ideas about it before you sit behind the wheel, look under the hood, or drive it on the highway.

This first reading will give you a general idea of where the course is heading. Study the overall unit goal and keep it in mind. Even if you are working with a teaching team that is creating its own curriculum, it is good to have a "big picture" as a general guide.

2. *Read the session.* Read the printed material that you will be using. Jot down ideas that pop into your head as you read. Remember that the printed curriculum is a guide. Most materials provide you with a teacher's manual, a student's book, and a resource packet for some age levels. Curriculum material must be written in a general way because it is distributed to a national market. It is your task as a teacher to fit the printed curriculum to the needs, skills, interests, and abilities of your students. You accomplish this by keeping the parts that fit well and by adapting and changing other parts—"tailoring" the material so that it fits your particular class. No one knows as much about your class as you, the teacher. Writers expect you to adapt their material to your class. In a sense, you are writing curriculum by fitting the material to your group.

Step 3: Last Week

Make a list of everything important that happened last week. Does anything that happened need follow-up this week? Did you make any promises that you must keep this week? Did you raise any expectations? Who was absent? Select some words that describe how you feel about what happened last week; for example, excited, happy, bored, up, down, determined.

Your list will furnish pointers for this session. For instance, when a student misses one Sunday (or several), you need to help him or her become a part of the class again. How can you help the student catch up and feel a sense of belonging? Keeping your list before you should influence your session planning, especially the opening activity. Place your label with your "last week" material.

Step 4: Concerns

Concerns are matters regarding members of your class, or the class as a whole, about which you intend to do something. Concerns can be identified as problems, needs, hurts, issues, suffering, opportunities, challenges, and hunches you have about your class. Teachers become aware of concerns by listening, observing, asking questions, and visiting in homes. Write out these concerns and keep them in mind as you do your session planning. A teacher's concern about something or someone can be active or passive. To be actively concerned means that you make some kind of response to the person's need, problem, or challenge. To be passively concerned means that you recognize the person's situation but choose not to respond to it.

What concerns came out of last week's session (or previous weeks')? What personal concerns exist within the group? Here are some possible concerns with examples of active and passive responses:

A young boy's story provides a clear description of both active and passive responses. Ron Kingbeil, thirteen years old and dying of leukemia, wrote the following letter to doctors and nurses. The Cadillac, Michigan, *Evening News* published it shortly before he died.

> "I am dying . . . No one likes to talk about such things. In fact, no one likes to talk about much at all . . . I am the one who is dying. I know you feel insecure, don't know what to say, don't know what to do. But please believe me, if you care, you can't go wrong. Just admit that you care. This is what we search for.

The Concern	*Passive Response*	*Active Response*
Joe was laid off last week.	You know about it but will ignore it in order not to embarrass Joe.	Express your concern to Joe. Pray for Joe and the family. Keep your ear open for job openings.
Susie (six years old) will have an operation this week. She's afraid.	Don't mention it because it will cause more fear and distrust. Pray for her privately.	Tell her you (or others from the class) will be in to see her. Pray for her in the class. Visit her.
Over half the class is coming late every Sunday.	Ignore it, or complain to the class. Make session plans accordingly.	Discuss it with the class. What are the reasons? Can anything be done about it? Check out expectations.

We may ask for whys and wherefores, but we really don't want answers. Don't run away. Wait. All I want to know is that there will be someone to hold my hand when I need it. I'm afraid . . . I've never died before . . ."

Even if you don't know how to put it into words exactly, let your students know that you care for them. This kind of active response allows your feelings to be communicated to the students. After you have made your list of concerns, identify the ones that need an active response this next Sunday and the ones that can wait. Also identify some possible responses. As you continue to plan your session, refer to this list of concerns from time to time. Now put your label on them.

Step 5: Unit Goal(s)

Most curriculum materials state at least one unit goal.[1] A unit of curriculum material usually covers thirteen weeks of sessions, or one quarter. A unit goal, then, is something you hope to accomplish over several months of teaching, not just one session.

In this book, goals are defined as

• long-range hopes, dreams, or visions; a true goal can take quite some time to achieve;

• general advice for teaching and making decisions;

• general statements that do not include a lot of details;

• descriptions of what will happen if the goals are accomplished, in other words, the product or the "end-state" (i.e., the hope, the dream, the outcome);

• realistic and achievable aims that nevertheless stretch people beyond normal accomplishments.

When you begin to teach a unit of curriculum, study the goal for the unit. After you have read the material, you may feel satisfied with the goal as it is written and proceed with your planning, using the goal statement. If you are not fully satisfied with the goal statement, you may want to modify it so that it more accurately reflects the needs of your class and what you want to accomplish through the unit. If you are completely dissatisfied with the goal statement, you may need to reject it and develop one or more of your own.

Goals can be shared with your class. It can be helpful for students to have an idea of what you hope to accomplish in a unit. As you gain more experience, you may want to involve your students in writing one or more unit goals related to the curriculum you are using. You and your students might also want to consider writing some goals that provide direction and challenge for a year of teaching and learning together. Classes of youth and adults, especially, are capable of identifying goals for the teaching/learning experience.

When you write a goal statement, begin with the word "that," followed by the person(s) who will try to reach the goal. Then use the word "be," which will describe something that has happened, is finished, or is completed. Complete the statement with what you hope will happen. Goal statements look something like the following:

"That my students be caring Christians in our classroom experience." A goal such as this might easily take more than one unit of teaching. It might take six months, a year, or even longer. A goal of this type will require many sessions of teaching and learning to achieve.

- "That my students be Christian in their everyday lives."
- "That my students be able to tell God's story in their daily lives."
- "That my students be kind to each other in their relationships both in and out of class."

All of these goal statements provide a challenge, something to strive for. You will make some progress toward achieving them in the course of teaching a unit, but most will take longer than that.

A teacher who has unit goals can have a "teaching disaster" on a given Sunday yet remain confident that all is not lost. There will be more Sundays when you can work to accomplish the goal, since you have not "put all your eggs in one basket."

Use the label to remind you of the importance of goal statements.

Step 6: Learning (Instructional) Objectives

Study your course material and decide what you want to work on for this session. Think about your concerns for your students and consider the focus of the written material. Then write clear, attainable objectives that grow out of steps 3, 4, and 5. There are two basic ways to write instructional objectives. One way is to write an objective or statement in terms of what the teacher is going to do. An illustration of this might be "To demonstrate to students how to tell God's story." This objective states what the teacher, not the student, is going to do. It would actually be possible to complete this demonstration and achieve the objective without the students having learned anything. This is not the correct way to write an objective.

The best way to write objectives is to specify the types of outcomes you expect to result from your teaching. Regarding the sample objective, the key question is, What can the students do after they have seen the demonstration? In other words, the focus of a learning objective should be directed toward student learning, not the teacher and the teaching activity. How you teach is not the point of the objective. Rather, what happens in the life of the student is the key. The key question is, What will the student be able to do or be? not, How did you teach the session?

A good objective includes an action verb. Some examples of appropriate verbs for writing objectives include the following:

Write	Find	Participate
Apply	Choose	Predict
Discuss	Decide	Explain
Collect	Copy	Attempt
Lead	Develop	Create
Design	Make	Locate
Paraphrase	Name	Compare
Give	Plan	Identify
Itemize	Use	Feel
Raise	Build	Share
Tell	Perform	Retell
Revise	List	Send
Color	Pick	Reproduce
Try	Finish	Save

As you observe your students, you will be able to determine whether these actions are taking place and, if so, how well. Action verbs give teachers clues about what is happening in the teaching/learning process in the classroom.

The best way to begin an objective is to state the time frame within which you will work. Good objectives contain time frames, at least one action verb, and what the student will be able to do, for example:

• At the end of today's session, the students will be able to *tell* one part of God's story.

• By the end of today's session, the students will have *decided* one part of God's story that they will share with someone else this week.

• At the conclusion of the next two sessions, the students will be able to *identify* some key parts of God's story.

• By the end of today's session, Mary, Mike, and Joanne will *work* as team teachers with me.

• Halfway through the session today, the class will *decide* which

part of God's story they want to dramatize in the second half of the
session.

• At the end of the first thirty minutes, the class will have
completed the collage.

As you continue to teach, you will discover that not every student
will fully meet your objectives every Sunday. Sometimes the entire
class will be able to accomplish an objective, sometimes half the
class, and there will no doubt be times when only a few will do so.
Many factors will influence the outcome. Be sure to evaluate what
each student does in response to an objective that wasn't met by the
whole class. Seek to determine if the students just had a bad day, if
all of you had a bad day, or if the objective was poorly written or
unfocused.

As you can see, learning objectives written in this manner will
help you determine very quickly if the learning you want to take
place is really happening. Clearly stated objectives are a key to
evaluation. Attach the label to your objectives.

Step 7: Session Outline

A session outline provides, at a quick glance, a look at the key
elements in the session. The key steps are laid out so that you can
see each one and its relationship to the next. Looking at the outline
is like looking at the skeleton of a large tree in winter. Because the
leaves are gone, you can clearly see the trunk and each of the large
branches.

At the beginning of your session outline, write down the number
of minutes you have to teach. If you are one of those fortunate
teachers who actually have sixty minutes of teaching time, begin
with that figure. If you don't have sixty minutes, indicate the actual
number of minutes you will have at the beginning of your session
outline. This target will determine to a large extent what you
can—and cannot—do. As you write out your outline, estimate a
length of time for each step or activity. Although it will only be a
"best guess," it will guide you in selecting appropriate activities.

Write down where your class will be meeting. In most cases, you
will meet in an assigned room. However, for special activities,

togetherness teaching, intergenerational experiences, or class exchanges, you may need time to move from place to place. Remember that whenever group movement occurs, even at the beginning of a session, you will sustain a loss of five to ten minutes in reestablishing the group, sometimes even longer.

A session outline is provided with most printed curriculum material. Study the printed suggestions. If you are satisfied with them, you may not have any other outlining to do. If the outline is not satisfactory, however, then you will need to create your own. When you have finished your outline, attach the label to it.

Some questions to ask in creating an outline are:

• How will I begin the session?

• What steps will I use for the heart of the session?

• What are the best ways to present the subject or main content of the session?

• What are some activities with which the class can explore the focus of the session?

• What are some ways in which students can respond?

• How will I close the session?

• What backup steps will I select and have ready for use if needed?

• What supplies or equipment are needed? Who will get them and set them up?

• Who on the teaching team is responsible for each part of the session?

These questions suggest teaching activities that will be dealt with in depth in chapter 4.

Step 8: Opening Activities

How you open your session usually determines what happens during the session. For instance, I once began a demonstration teaching session with youth and adult observers in a weekend lab by pretending to be an atheist. I threw the Bible on the floor and told them that was what I thought about "their" Bible. The Bible was immediately rescued by one of the teens, and the session was well on its way. This activity took no more than thirty seconds, but it brought every person into the session immediately.

Obviously, a teacher can't use such a dramatic opening activity every Sunday, but once in a while it may help to begin with a "flare" of activity. Your students, whether children, youth, or adult, are TV viewers. If a program doesn't hold the viewer's attention for the first two or three minutes, the person will probably switch the channel. You can't compete with the visual interest of television, but you can make your sessions interesting, exciting, and attractive. Opening activities may include:

• Sharing among class members. What has happened to us since we last met? (This should be a guided discussion about what has happened to individuals while the class has been separated.)

• Current issues at school, community, work, etc.

• Scripture (should be handled creatively when used as the opening activity).

• Something left over from the last session.

• Media, such as videos, television, cassettes.

• Making a decision about something the class would like to do.

• A brief visit from the pastor or someone else who can "set the stage" for the session.

• Making plans for a future program, togetherness teaching, or other activity.

• Magazines and local newspapers. Almost every session you teach will make use of illustrative material that students have read about in the local newspaper or have heard about in some other way. Youth classes can be enlisted to collect items from school bulletin boards that refer to the session—great team teaching!

• Starting the session with a debate. Set up two sides to debate the issue or subject.

• Interest centers, learning centers.

You need to decide how much time you can give to the opening activity. It can be merged with another step in the session; it need not be completely separated from everything else you do in the session. Place your label with the opening activity.

Step 9: Teaching Activities

Select the teaching activities that most effectively facilitate accomplishing your learning objectives. There are many from which to choose. A general approach to the subject of teaching methods is Martha M. Leypoldt's book *40 Ways to Teach in Groups*.[3] It contains descriptions, diagrams, and illustrations of a wide variety of teaching methods.

The time you spend on learning about and selecting the best teaching activities is time well spent. A good selection of a variety of teaching methods and activities is one of the best ways to keep sessions interesting and keep students involved.

The subject of teaching activities is much too broad to cover in detail here. The primary source for teaching activities is the curriculum you are teaching. A basic assumption on which you can normally depend is that the writers of a curriculum are not only most knowledgeable of the subject, but are well aware of the interests and characteristics of the age-level group for whom it is being written. It is important to seriously consider suggestions found in your curriculum. Beyond that, be creative in using your own gifts and skills, and as well, borrow ideas from daily life and any other sources available to you.

Step 10: Closing Activities

A closing activity is appropriate for most sessions. Closing activities may be used to tie the session together, deal with relationships and feelings within the group, or introduce a separate activity. Sometimes the involvement of students and teacher in a session is so intense that there is no time for a closing activity. This may leave students with confused, unsettled feelings. Therefore it is usually best to include some kind of closing activity. Some possible closing activities may include

- sharing what class members have learned and any commitments they have made,
- making creative use of Scripture and prayer,
- bridging class experience to morning worship experience,

- singing together,
- listening to appropriate contemporary music,
- praying together individually, in small groups, or as the complete group,
- writing out prayers,
- celebrating with a miniparty,
- making some agreements and commitments for the next session,
- previewing highlights of the next session to whet class members' appetite,
- making decisions about projects,
- evaluation,
- summarizing the session in a meaningful, creative way,
- creating your own closing activity.

When you have chosen your closing activities, attach your label to the list.

Step 11: Participation

Although not a true step, student participation is so important that it must receive special attention in planning. Participation is related directly to the activities used to teach the session. It is important to design participation into your session plan. Look for it. Be sure it is there.

Participation is the key to the learning experience. Students today expect to participate. The day of the classroom lecture is over. If the church school is to be a vital part of a local church's ministry, it must discover the keys to meaningful participation.

Participation does not mean "busywork." Many teachers, pressed for time, judge a curriculum by its "busywork." Participation calls for the student's involvement in the session. Participation is the student's response to the content, both as a receiver and a responder. Students can participate in every phase of the session if the teacher plans well. This includes participation from the time the session is on the "drawing board" through final evaluation.

Participation activities should be varied. One lesson we can learn from television is that variety is essential. People today live with and expect constant change. Our church schools should offer variety to students of all ages as they participate in Christian learning.

Teaching that provides little student participation takes less time to prepare than teaching that uses a variety of teaching activities. However, the results of student participation make the additional time very worthwhile. Use the label to remind you of the value of participation.

Step 12: Materials and Resources

Your session plan will call for the use of selected materials and resources. Some of these need to be secured well in advance of the Sunday they are to be used; others can be collected quickly and easily. Make a list of the materials you need, when you will need them, how they will be secured, and by whom. Students of any age level can assist in gathering materials. One problem can occur when you delegate—the student may not follow through with the task. A last-minute check should be made in order to be certain that you will have what you are expecting each person to bring. If you don't check, you may be disappointed when you learn that you can't carry out a part of your session plan. Put your label on your list.

Step 13: Evaluation

Evaluation means considering carefully the worth or value of what you have done. In teaching, it includes both teacher and student views of what happened. In most cases, evaluation is a process used to measure something against a standard. Your *standards* will be found in the *learning objectives* you wrote for the session.

Evaluation takes place in a number of ways, including reflection on what happened; student feedback to the teacher on what they felt, observed, and learned; review; recall; feelings; dialogue; summaries; and written comments. Some good general questions to ask at the conclusion of a session or unit are:

• What happened?
• Was it what you wanted to have happen?

• Did enough happen to make the class worthwhile to the students and the teaching team (or teacher)?
  • What worked really well?
  • What should have been done differently in terms of an opening activity, teaching activities, room arrangements, resources, or closing activities?
There are several sources from which to make your evaluation. They include
  • you, the teacher,
  • other members of your teaching team,
  • students in the class,
  • the class as a whole,
  • parents.
When the session is over and you've had an opportunity to reflect on it briefly, an organized approach to evaluation is most helpful. Here are three basic questions to help organize your thinking about what happened as a result of the session.

1. How well did you organize to teach the session? You may recall that in chapter 1, one of the teacher's roles was to be an organizer. How well did you organize your session outline? Did you make all the necessary arrangements for materials and resources? Did you write out your objectives and ask questions about them for review? Did you take care of the details that made (or could have made) the session a success?

2. How well did things go? This question refers to the process. Do you feel that the whole teaching experience went smoothly? Did the opening activities flow smoothly into the next step? Did the teaching activities you selected blend well with other steps?

3. Did anything happen to or for the students? This is the "product," the end result. Did the learning objectives produce results? Were the students equipped to do what you wanted them to be able to do by the end of the session? the end of the unit? the end of the month? What happened that makes you think you accomplished your objective(s)?

Evaluation may be the most important step in teaching. There are two basic benefits for the teacher from regular evaluation.

1. Affirmation for what you are doing. If you do a good job, it is

satisfying to know this directly from your students, their parents, or peers. Encouragement and support from your class are necessary components of the teaching process. Each teacher should know when the job is done well!

2. Sensitivity to what is happening. There are no perfect teachers, perfect students, or perfect sessions. There is always room for improvement in teaching/learning experiences. The process of evaluation often provides clues to what is working well, as well as what isn't working.

Evaluation is a positive, supportive step and should not be considered a threatening experience. The label will remind you of this final step.

Notes

1. Various publishers, curriculum writers, educators, etc., attach different meanings to the term "goal," so be sure to note what it means in the curriculum you are using. It will be defined very early in the unit material.

2. Martha M. Leypoldt, *40 Ways to Teach in Groups*, rev. ed. (Valley Forge, Pa.: Judson, 1992). As you read educational periodicals, be alert for articles on new teaching activities. When you have determined which teaching activities you will use, place your label with them.

Chapter 4

Teaching Activities

Teaching activities are methods of teaching that the teacher uses to bring the content and the student together. Donald L. Griggs suggests several useful criteria for deciding which teaching activities to employ.

1. The activity should involve most of the students in an active way.

2. It should be an activity that the teacher has some confidence in.

3. It should allow for maximum creative input from the students.

4. It should not be so familiar that it bores the students.

5. If the activity is new, students should have the opportunity to experiment with it in order to discover its possibilities.

6. A variety of activities should be offered so that students have a choice.

7. The activity should directly support the key points of the lesson and should contribute to achieving the learning objectives.

8. The activity should lead the students to seek answers, state conclusions, or express creative responses.

9. Whatever activities are designed should be appropriate to the ages and skills of the students involved.[1]

Student learning and teaching activities are interrelated. They must be considered together if effective learning is to take place. Let's take another look at Leypoldt's list of the ways in which learning takes place from *40 Ways to Teach in Groups*.

Learning takes place when the following changes occur:

1. Information is added.
2. Understanding is increased.
3. New attitudes are accepted.
4. New appreciations are acquired.
5. What has been learned is used actively.

These five kinds of changes fall into the three categories of knowing, feeling, and doing. The categories consist of:

1. What I add to what I already know.
2. How I feel about what I hear and read.
3. What I do with what I hear and read.[2]

Your task as teacher is to bring together the content and the learner. The key question is, What is the best way to do this? Most of the curriculum material you will use provides suggestions for teaching activities, including various ways to present certain parts of the session. You can find additional suggestions from other teachers, training experiences, resource books, age-level magazines and journals, and your own previous experiences. The teacher's task is to identify the best teaching activities for the class.

If adding information is one of your learning objectives for your students, what is the best way to present this information to them? If you wish to create new or change existing student attitudes, what is the best way (method or activity) to do this?

If another of your learning objectives is to have students do something with what they have learned, what is the best way to bring it about? Obviously, there is more than one way to accomplish each objective. The key question is, Which method is best for *your* students?

Here is a list of factors to consider as you choose teaching activities.

1. The Class
• What is the size of the class?
• What is the age range of class members?
• What is the male-female ratio?
• What are attendance patterns—regular? irregular? seasonal?
• Who was present and who was absent last week?
• Who comes early and who comes late?

• What are the attitudes of the students—eager? lazy? curious? ambitious? creative? we care? we don't care? traditional?

• What is the climate? (Factors that combine to create a climate within a class include culture, sociology, traditions, education, race, age range, spiritual background, and heritage.)

2. The Room

• Is ample space available for class activities that call for movement, groups, etc.?

• Is your space limited? Is the furniture movable or stationary?

• Is the room cheery, bright, and warm?

• Do you and the students feel good about the room?

• Is the room fairly soundproof? How close is your classroom to other classes? (The closeness of other classes may have some bearing on your selection of teaching activities.)

3. Time

• How many minutes of actual teaching time do you have?

4. Learning Objectives

• What do your objectives say about the teaching activities you will use?

5. Resources

• What materials, resources, equipment, or settings are required for the teaching activities you'd like to use?

• Do you have them? If not, can you get them?

6. The Teacher

• What do you like to do? What are your interests, hobbies, skills, likes, and dislikes?

Eventually these factors become part of your personal knowledge and resources, and you can make use of them as needed. As you get to know your students personally and gain experience and confidence in teaching, your selection process will take these factors into consideration intuitively. You won't have to go over the checklist every time you select teaching activities.

Steps to Take in Selecting Teaching Activities

What considerations do you take into account first in choosing teaching activities? There is an order that, if observed, is helpful.

1. Which teaching activities/methods do you like best? How open are you to considering new and different teaching methods?

2. What do your students like doing? What do they dislike? How open is your class to doing some things differently?

3. What is the session about? What are the key points or concepts suggested in the curriculum material?

4. What are your learning objectives?

5. What did you do last week? What teaching activities did you use? List.

6. Brainstorm a number of ways to teach the various parts of the session. Which are best?

7. How many do you need? Narrow the list to the best two or three.

8. Make your final decision.

Here is a sample first-person illustration of how this works. Put yourself in the place of this teacher, who has a class of adults. This is what the teacher considered when selecting teaching activities.

1. My favorite methods of teaching include several types of participation activities and audiovisuals. I'm a little afraid to try a lot of new activities.

2. My adult class is content to sit and listen to me talk to them. They aren't very eager to be engaged in activities during the session. My guess is that I may be able to involve them in one or two new teaching activities, but I will have to move slowly.

3. The session is about witnessing—telling God's story. The main points include *(a)* the story I have to tell; *(b)* those who need to hear the story; *(c)* how to tell the story so that others will understand it.

4. My two learning objectives for this session call for involving students in witnessing about their faith at home and at work.

• By the end of the session, each student *will decide* which part of God's story he or she can tell best.

• By the end of the session, each student will be able to *decide* where he or she can tell a part of the story during the next week or so.

5. Last week we discussed the session as a total group. I provided input for about ten minutes and then attempted to get the students

to talk with other students as well as with me. We were somewhat successful. They were still much more willing to talk back and forth with me, the teacher, than with each other.

6. The activities that I could use include lecturing; paired discussion; having the pairs decide what parts of God's story each student can share; making lists with the total group; a video on the first chapter of Acts; demonstrating a real-life witnessing situation to the class; inviting the pastor to share with us a recent witnessing experience. I think the best methods are:

• demonstrating witnessing to the class,
• deciding in pairs what parts of God's story each will share,
• sharing lists with the entire class and making a decision.

7. These three activities will best fit the time we have. I'd like to see the video but don't believe there will be time for it.

8. These three are the best of the activities listed in item 6.

Space does not permit considering all the possible teaching activities for all age groups. Leypoldt's book provides an excellent overview of many ways to teach or work with groups. The beginning chapters also provide a good understanding of group dynamics.

In this book, space allows a separate presentation for only three different methods of teaching. Each illustration provided will be for a different age group. The theme and Scripture for each will be the same.

Illustration 1: Adult Class

The setting: An adult class with one teacher.

Session title and theme: "You will be my witnesses" (Acts 1:1-11; read this Scripture before proceeding with the chapter).

The class: The adult class is composed of twenty-two persons (on the roll) with an average attendance of twelve to fourteen persons. Members' ages range from twenty-six to fifty-five. There are married couples, single adults without children, and single adults with children. Almost all members of the class, both male and female, are employed outside the home.

The room: The class meets in the sanctuary. The pews are stationary. There are no tables.

The time: Fifty minutes of actual teaching time is available.

Session Plan
Step 1: Prayer

"Lord God, first I pray for myself, for I greatly need your presence with me. By myself I will not accomplish very much. But if you will guide and support me, I may be able to help these students. Help me to plan. Help me to think clearly. Help me to listen to each person; may I be able to understand what they are really saying to me and to each other.

"I pray for each member in the class. Please be with Jim as he goes into the hospital next week. And thanks so much for healing Mary . . . we love her so much. Margaret and Joe are hurting a lot; please be a meaningful presence to them right now. And Joe needs a job, God. Help us all to keep looking for something for him. Now help me with this session, God. I'm open to your guidance as I plan. And help me when I get together with the class. Don't leave me alone, please. In the name of Jesus. Amen."

Step 2: Reading

Read the unit and the session material. The unit goal is "to be informed about the early church's first months of ministry, as recorded in the first eight chapters of the book of Acts."

Step 3: Last Week

Some students became involved; others didn't participate. It was Mary's first time back after her operation. Everyone was glad to see her and made her feel very welcome. Jim enters the hospital on Monday. We're all concerned about what he faces. I tried to persuade the students to work on a collage as a concluding activity for the last unit, but to no avail. I was angry with the class. Yet all seemed to be eager to start studying the new unit in the book of Acts; in fact, several seem to be excited about it. The sanctuary was cold. Nine persons were absent; six for the first time. Two persons have missed two consecutive Sundays, and one has not showed up for three consecutive weeks. I must visit him at home this week. (Note: Here is a guide for you to follow concerning student absences: one absence, a card is sent; two absences, a phone call is made; three consecutive absences are followed by a personal visit.)

Step 4: Concerns

Sam has been absent for three consecutive Sundays. Jim enters the hospital on Monday with some serious health problems. Margaret and Joe's two teens refuse to come to church school. Their parents are deeply hurt by their refusal. Sue, Mark, and Max seem ready to participate if someone will help them. Jerry is still unemployed—we need to watch the extra offerings. As far as I can tell, most class members are extremely shy about witnessing (verbally) to others about their faith.

Step 5: Unit Goal

I have two goals for this unit:
1. That my students will have a greater knowledge of the need for individual Christians to witness about their faith.
2. That each member of the class will be willing to witness in at least one new place in his or her everyday life.

Step 6: Learning Objectives

I have three learning objectives.
1. By the end of the session, each student will have *shared* with at least one other student a meaningful part of his or her faith story.
2. By the end of the session, each student will *know the meaning* of Jesus' words before his ascension, "You shall be my witnesses."
3. By the end of the session, each student will be able to *decide* where daily witnessing can take place in his or her life.

Step 7: Session Outline (50 minutes)

Opening activity: Interacting with the Scripture passage in a new way.

The heart of the session: Working on a definition of witness. What do we witness about?

The urgency of witnessing: That witnessing be seen as an opportunity rather than as a demand.

Closing activity: Sharing and decision making about witnessing.

Step 8: Opening Activities (8 minutes)

Read the first eleven verses of Acts 1 in a fresh way. Ask several persons, in advance, to read the different characters in the passage, including

- narrator (verses 1-5, 9-10),
- disciples (verse 6),
- Jesus (verses 7-8),
- two men (verse 11).

We will read this passage from three different versions of the Bible so that students will taste the different flavor in each: the King James Version, the *New Revised Standard Version,* and the *Good News Bible.*

I will call four persons early in the week to read the different parts. We'll get together to rehearse about ten minutes before the class starts.

Step 9: Teaching Activities (31 minutes)

1. Group sharing. What do we know about the book of Acts? On newsprint (or chalkboard) list all the contributions from the class. Do not discuss them as they are given. Enlist one of the students to write on the newsprint. (8 minutes)

2. The meaning of the word "witness," the word "share," and the term "God's story." Use pictures from contemporary magazines or newspapers in which some type of witnessing or sharing is shown, or some part of God's story is acted out. In advance, mark each picture with "witnessing," "sharing," or "a part of God's story." Divide the class into pairs and give each pair a picture. Ask each student to share with his or her partner what the picture suggests about witnessing or sharing, or what part of God's story is portrayed. Almost every advertisement or commercial is a "witness" or "testimony" to what the company hopes to sell! (8 minutes)

3. Invite someone to visit the class who has a personal illustration to share about one of the three terms. Perhaps Mary would have a

story to tell about sharing that came out of her recent hospital experience. I will also prepare a personal illustration to use as a backup if time permits. (6 minutes)

4. Move the students back to the same pairings. Ask them to share with each other which part of God's story they would be willing to witness about and in what settings of their everyday life this could take place. (9 minutes)

Step 10: Closing Activity (5 minutes)

Ask one or two members of the class to share briefly their favorite part of God's story and where they can best be a witness to it.

Step 11: Participation

Student participation is suggested at several points:
- group sharing about the book of Acts
- using pictures in pairs
- sharing about witnessing in pairs
- closing activity of sharing
- evaluation

Step 12: Materials and Resources

1. Newsprint stand, newsprint, and marker (or chalkboard and chalk)

2. Pictures from magazines and newspapers

3. Three versions of the Bible for the readers

4. Pencils (or pens) for evaluation

Step 13: Evaluation (5-6 minutes)

This is the first session of a new unit. Ask each pair to write their feelings about the session on the picture they discussed. Ask if they have gained a new or a greater understanding of Jesus' last words to his followers. How willing—or unwilling—are they to be witnesses? Use only one or two "feeling" words. Leave the pictures at the end of the pews as they leave. Close with a prayer that mentions Jim's admission to the hospital tomorrow.

Later, check out the learning objectives. Did I accomplish all of them or some of them? How well? Did I observe all class members participating in pairs? Did some not know how to work in pairs? Did some refuse to participate at all? What did I observe in the fifty minutes about the teaching activities I selected? *End of session.*

Key Questions for the Reader to Ask

1. What might the students have learned?

2. Could the three learning objectives have been accomplished (step 6)?

3. Could two-way communication take place?

4. Did anything happen that might have contributed to accomplishing the unit goal?

5. How might the teacher have felt about what happened?

6. How might the students have felt about what happened?

7. Did the teacher follow the session plan? If not, where and why were adjustments made?

8. What points should be noted for next week's session planning?

9. What types of participation and communication flow do you see illustrated in this session plan? The following diagrams illustrate what was hoped would happen.

**CODE: T—TEACHER   S—STUDENT
N—NEWSPRINT (OR CHALKBOARD)**

STEP 8—OPENING ACTIVITY

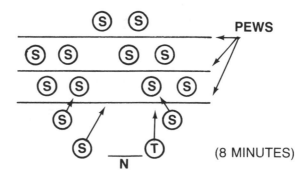

PEWS

(8 MINUTES)

STEP 9—TEACHING ACTIVITIES

#1

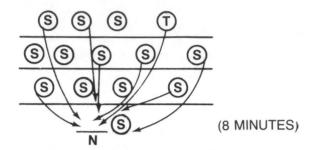

(8 MINUTES)

#2

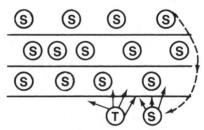

(8 MINUTES)

#3

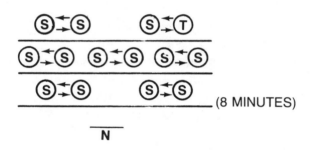

(6 MINUTES)

#4

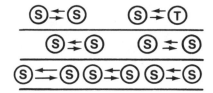

(9 MINUTES)

A final question: Based on the information you have been given, did this teacher actually accomplish the learning objectives? If not, what could the teacher have done to facilitate accomplishing the objectives? Remember that this teacher has to function in a sanctuary setting, not a separate classroom. Do you feel the session plan was carefully worked through and that it was realistic?

Illustration 2: Senior High Class

The setting: A senior high class with team teachers, each with equal responsibility.

Session title or theme: "You shall be my witnesses" (Acts 1:1-11).

The class: The senior high class is composed of eleven teens in grades nine through twelve. There are seven girls and four boys. Average attendance is eight. Some Sundays only three or four are present, while on other Sundays the whole class attends. Over half the students have part-time jobs, and several of them work on Saturday night. Some students always arrive late. Three girls leave a few minutes early to join the adult choir.

The room: The classroom is separate and has one door and two windows. There is a rug on the floor; there are two tables and a chalkboard. The room has good lighting. However, it is rather small; this factor limits the range of activities.

The time: Fifty minutes of actual teaching time is available, although the latecomers and the early departers reduce that by about ten minutes.

Session Plan
Step 1: Prayer

"Lord God, this is a beautiful bunch of kids we have to teach. I'm not sure we're capable of doing the job, but we're willing to give it a try. They say some of the craziest things, and it's hard sometimes to know what they're saying to us. Help us to keep right on listening in the hope that we will hear what they really want to say to us. We need to be patient—help us, God! And help my teaching partner to accept me for what I am and to understand me as well. God, I really want to love each of these teens—please help me to do it. Please help us as we plan this session—we can't do it alone. Help us make it better than the last one. We thank you for the promise that you'll be with us. In Jesus' name. Amen.

"God, our Father, help us with this job of teaching. You know we didn't ask to do this; but here we are, and we need your help. Help us plan this session. Something went wrong last week, God, and we want to make this one better. So bless us as we try again. The kids say they like us, God, and that means a lot. May they know we love them too.

"Please give a special blessing to Joanne, Marian, Matt, Jean, Millie, and Dee—they're all great, God—bless each member of the class. Help me to be patient, loving, and kind no matter what happens. Most of all, help me not to get mad at them or to speak sharply. Help me to develop my teaching skills, God. I really want to do this. Thanks for listening to us. In Christ's name. Amen."

Step 2: Reading

We have already read the material for the session. The unit goal is "to gain knowledge of the early church's first months of ministry through the first eight chapters of the book of Acts."

Step 3: Last Week

Nine were present. Six were on time and three were late. We tried to highlight the next session in an exciting way. They seemed to be interested in what we were suggesting for next week. There was a big basketball game on Saturday (we lost). After class, two of the girls told us that Mike is using drugs from time to time. Joanne insists on getting married before she finishes high school. Sam is "wild" because he turns sixteen next week and will be able to get his driver's license. Our session plan didn't work out very well last week. They were hard on us in the evaluation, but they insist that they love us very much, regardless of how the session turns out.

Step 4: Concerns

Marian has missed three consecutive Sundays. Joanne is worried about being pregnant. Matt has been seen driving recklessly and was almost involved in several accidents. Jean, Millie, and Dee seem to be growing in their faith—how can we help them further? How can we make this unit about witnessing for Christ real for the teens in our class?

Step 5: Unit Goal

That our students will be better prepared as individual Christians to witness to their faith.

Step 6: Learning Objectives

1. By the end of today's session, each student will have *shared* with at least one other person some meaningful part of his or her faith story.

2. By the end of the session, each student will be able to *recount* the ascension story as recorded in Acts 1:1-11.

3. By the end of today's session, each student will have *decided* on one part of his or her life where witness can take place.

Step 7: Session Outline (50 minutes total)

Opening activity: Approaching the Scripture passage in an original way.

The heart of the session: Working at defining witness, acting out witnessing, and deciding what it is that witnesses for Christ tell about.

Closing activity: Sharing and decision making about witnessing.

Step 8: Opening Activity (5 minutes)

Group reading of the first eleven verses of Acts 1. Ask several
teens, in advance, to read the different verses for the characters in
the story, including
- narrator (verses 1-5; 9-10),
- disciples (verse 6),
- Jesus (verses 7-8),
- two men (verse 11).

Read the verses from three different versions—the King James
Version, *Good News for Modern Man,* and the *New Revised Standard Version.* Call four teens in advance to take the four parts; ask
them to come ten minutes before class starts to rehearse the reading.
Encourage them to put some expression into reading their parts.

Code: T—Teacher   S—Student

STEP 8—OPENING ACTIVITY

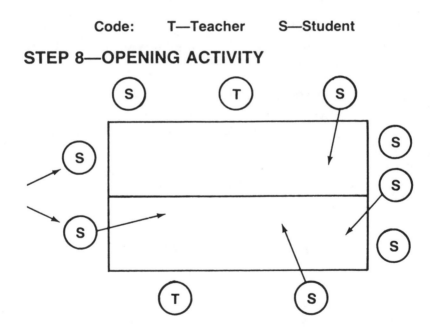

Step 9: Teaching Activities (43 minutes)

1. Introduce the book of Acts with a twelve-minute video. Ask Mary and Sue to show the video. Provide an overview of the study unit on witnessing. (15 minutes)

2. Discuss as a group what it means to be a witness. Ask these questions:

- When, during this past week, did you witness something?
- What does it mean to be a witness in court?
- What does it mean to be a witness on the international scene, considering persons in refugee camps, persons starving anywhere in the world, bombings, killings, etc. (10 minutes)

3. What is the Christian faith to which we are witnesses? Offer one or two statements; then involve students in discussion. After a few minutes, suggest making banners on which some "witness" phrases or words that they choose can be placed. The banners could then be paraded before, during, or after a worship service sometime in the future. The class needs to consult with the proper board or worship committee as to the best time and manner for this witness to the congregation. Seek consensus from the class. (10 minutes)

4. In pairs, briefly share what part of God's story they like best and feel they can share. (8 minutes)

Step 10: Closing Activity (2 minutes)

The pairs join hands and pray for each other as they try to witness this week. The prayers can be verbal or silent.

Step 11: Participation

Students may participate in
- reading Scripture,
- showing a video,
- sharing what it means to be a witness,
- decision making about banners,
- sharing a part of God's story with another,
- praying for each other.

CODE: T—TEACHER   S—STUDENT

STEP 9—TEACHING ACTIVITIES

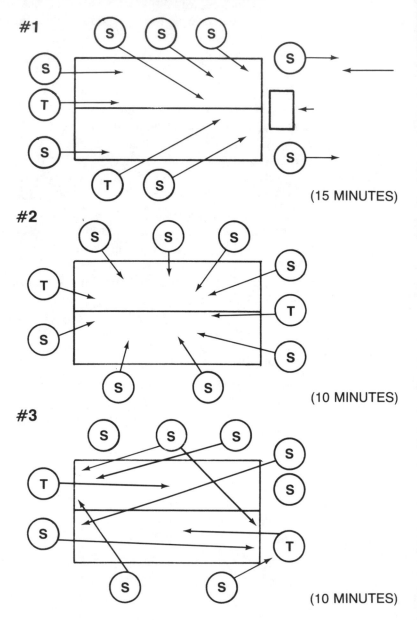

#1

(15 MINUTES)

#2

(10 MINUTES)

#3

(10 MINUTES)

STEP 9—TEACHING ACTIVITIES (CONTINUED)

#4

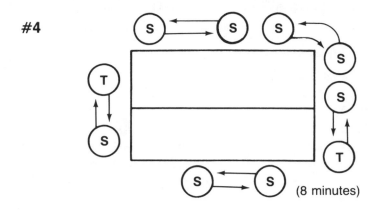

(8 minutes)

STEP 10—CLOSING ACTIVITY

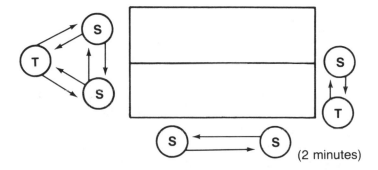

(2 minutes)

Step 12: Materials and Resources

1. Three different versions of the Bible for each reading
2. A video and video equipment
3. A sample banner or picture of a banner to give them ideas for their own banner

Step 13: Evaluation

Since we won't have but a minute, we'll do a quick evaluation. As the class leaves, we'll ask for a "thumbs up-thumbs down" evaluation. Thumbs up means it was really great! Hands level means it was so-so. Thumbs down means it wasn't so great. (These are teens, and evaluation can be fun while also providing them with a quick and easy way to express their feelings.) *End of session.*

Key Questions for the Reader to Ask:

1. What might the students have learned?

2. Could the three learning objectives have been accomplished (step 6)?

3. Could two-way communication take place?

4. Could something happen that would have provided movement toward the unit goal?

5. How might the teacher feel about what was planned and what happened?

6. How might the students feel about what happened, especially in light of a less-than-positive experience the week before?

7. Did the teachers follow the session plan? If not, where and why were adjustments made?

8. What points should be noted for next week's session planning?

The participation and communication flow in illustration 2 differs somewhat from illustration 1. On pages 74, 76, and 77 are diagrams meant to help you see the flow.

Did these teachers actually accomplish the learning objectives, based on the plan set before you? If not, what could the teacher have changed to accomplish the objectives? What do you think could have gone wrong in this session plan? Do you feel the teachers had a good attitude toward their students? Do you feel their session plan was carefully worked out? Was it realistic?

Illustration 3: Primary Class

The setting: A primary class with two team teachers and an assistant.

Session title or theme: "You will be my witnesses" (Acts 1:1-11).

The class: The primary class includes first, second, and third graders. There are twenty members in the class—twelve girls and eight boys. Average attendance is fourteen. The children are of average intelligence and ability. Four children live in single-parent homes; the others have intact families. Most of the children have attended a church school for several years. Three children have moved into the area during the last six months.

The room: The class meets in a rather large classroom that has its own sink, refrigerator, and toilet. The room has several offset areas where small clusters of children can gather. A large rug covers much of the floor. There are smaller rugs in other areas. Furniture is suitable for children of this age and size. An assortment of supplies and equipment is kept in cupboards in the room. A number of windows provide plenty of natural light. Good lighting exists otherwise.

The teachers: A team of two teachers meets regularly to plan and teach this class. A volunteer assistant is available on Sunday mornings, although this person does not have the time to become more involved with the team. The team meets in person at least once every two weeks. Two sessions are planned at each planning session. When time permits, the team meets every week, but the current practice seems to meet the teachers' needs.

The time: Fifty minutes of actual teaching time are available.

Session Plan
Step 1: Prayer

"Lord God, I pray for my teaching partner and for myself too. Help us as we plan together. You know it's difficult to find the amount of time needed to do good planning. We're trying, God, and we pray for your help to make it all worthwhile. Help me to listen to my partners and to each of the children. Sometimes, God, I know what I want them all to do, and they don't do it. Forgive me when I hurry, when I'm angry, or when I panic. Teach me to be patient with myself first and then with my partners and the children. Guide our thinking as we plan now, God. And thank you. Amen.

"Thank you, Lord God, for such good teaching partners. Sometimes we wonder if we know what we're doing, but, God, we know you are in this with us. And that makes a good team. Bless Annie who works with us faithfully every Sunday morning. She has a hard life, God; please bless her in a special way for her willingness to do anything that she is asked. God, please bless each of the children.

I'll try to remember all of their names—Ann, Jane, Martha, Kate, John, Jim, Mike, Walt, Bud, Marcy, Winnie, Virginia, Jan, Mary Beth, Margaret, Russ, David, Barb, Marie, and Carl. Each child is precious, God, so help us do the best job we possibly can. And please bless all their parents too. Our session is about witnessing. Help us to witness when we teach. Help us to plant some seeds in their young lives so that they will be witnesses. We believe this is important work, God, so please be with us right through this class. We thank you for this opportunity to *teach*. In Christ's name. Amen."

Step 2: Reading

All of us have read the unit and the first session.

Step 3: Last Week

Thirteen children were present. Our team of three teachers was present, and all arrived ten minutes before starting time. Eight children were present on time; five were late.

The session went well. We completed all the teaching activities. We also evaluated the unit, and the children seem to have learned quite a bit. This was a good session.

The children seem to be interested in the new unit. Although they don't know much about the book of Acts, they are willing to "give it a try."

Step 4: Concerns

Marcy is irritable most of the time, even when other children try to be nice to her. Jim and Jan (brother and sister) have missed two consecutive Sundays. Mary Beth has been absent three Sundays. Kate talks about her mom and dad fighting "all the time." Martha is afraid to go to school. Walt isn't doing well at school. Margaret seems to be ill much of the time. Carl needs a lot of loving. David is very disruptive.

Step 5: Unit Goal

The unit goal as stated in the curriculum is "be familiar with the details of the early church's first months of existence as recorded in the first eight chapters of the book of Acts." We changed the goal to read "that the children in our class be aware that Jesus has asked all of us to be his witnesses."

Step 6: Learning Objectives

We have two learning objectives.

1. By the end of the session, each student will be able to *know* what Jesus meant by the word "witness."

2. Before the class goes home, each student will have *participated* in at least one activity in which witnessing is communicated.

Step 7: Session Outline (50 minutes total)

Opening activity: Involve children with posters and pictures; invite a guest to tell a story about witnessing.

The heart of the session: Read the Scripture; involve the children in several activities; talk together about being a witness.

Closing activity: Focus on what it means to be a witness to brothers and sisters, mothers and fathers.

Step 8: Opening Activities (10 minutes)

Hang several pictures and posters in conspicuous places. The pictures and posters should depict persons or animals looking at something or perhaps looking at each other (such as a zoo scene). Include the word "witness" in big letters above and around the picture or poster. As children arrive, guide them in small groups from picture to picture. Talk with them about what they see and about what those in the pictures or posters are looking at.

We know we will have latecomers. The children arriving late will not see the pictures because children and teachers will have taken them down. Ask the children who have seen the pictures to try to remember what they saw, since they will be asked to be "witnesses" about these pictures later.

When all children have arrived, pause for a prayer.

Step 9: Teaching Activities (30 minutes)

1. Invite someone (preferably one of the children's parents) to visit the class and tell a personal story of an experience being a

witness to something. If possible, the story should illustrate something witnessed when he or she was a child. Listen to the story. Let the children ask questions of the storyteller. Be sure they understand who the witness was, what was witnessed (seen), and what it means to be a witness. Then the visitor leaves. (10 minutes)

2. Share the Scripture verse from Acts 1:8: "You will be my witnesses." Ask the question, What did Jesus mean? Show the children the verse written on a large piece of newsprint. Share with them that Jesus included each child when he said this. Tell them about the three learning center activities they can now choose. (5 minutes)

3. Set up three learning center activity areas. Each center will offer a different experience to the children, and each will focus on witnessing. Each member of the teaching team will work at one of the centers. (15 minutes)

• Use drama and role play to answer the question asked of children who go to church and church school, What do you do there? Help the children answer this question by role playing and by dramatizing some of the things they do at church and in church school.

• Make a collage that answers the question, How does a church witness? Help the children select and prepare pictures for placement in the collage.

• This learning center will deal with the question, How do I invite another person to come to church or church school? The children at this center will be challenged to invite another child to join them next Sunday. Role play how to extend the invitation, what to say, how to help new children enjoy church school, and so forth.

Step 10: Closing Activity (10 minutes)

Identify those who didn't see the pictures at the beginning of the class. Then ask how many "witnessed" the pictures. Ask these children to share what they saw with those who did not see them. Explain that they are being witnesses as they share what they saw. Make a circle and close the class session with a brief prayer.

Step 11: Participation

The children will participate
- at the opening picture activity,
- by listening to the story told by the visitor,
- by sharing the Scripture verse,
- at the three learning center activities,
- by sharing what they saw in the pictures/posters.

Step 12: Materials and Resources

1. Pictures and posters
2. A person to tell a story about witnessing
3. Materials for learning centers

Step 13: Evaluation (5-6 minutes)

This is the beginning session in the unit. You will find helpful a participation chart of the learning center activity. (See page 116 for instructions on how to complete and use a participation chart.) Since each teacher will have a specific responsibility at a center, we will ask the departmental superintendent to join us during that time period and do a participation chart of one of the centers of activity. *End of session.*

Key Questions for the Reader to Use

1. What might the students have learned?
2. Could the two learning objectives have been accomplished using this session plan (step 6)?
3. Could two-way communication take place?
4. Did anything happen that might have helped the teachers work toward accomplishing the unit goal?
5. How might the teachers feel about what happened?
6. How might the students have felt about what happened at the completion of the class session?
7. Did the teachers follow the session plan? If not, where and why did they make adjustments?
8. What points should be noted for next week's session planning?

This third illustration offers even more communication and

STEP 8—OPENING ACTIVITY

CODE: T—TEACHER   S—STUDENT

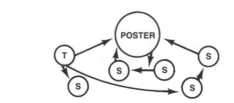

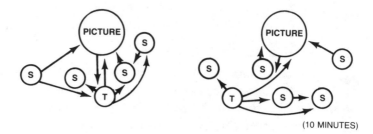

(10 MINUTES)

CODE: T—TEACHER   S—STUDENT   V—VISITOR

STEP 9—TEACHING ACTIVITIES

#1

(10 MINUTES)

#2

(15 MINUTES)

#3

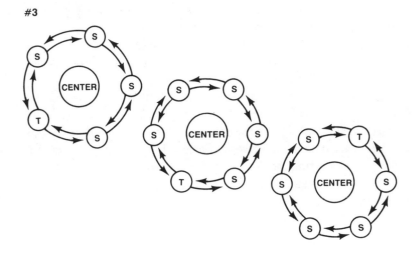

STEP 10—CLOSING ACTIVITY

#1

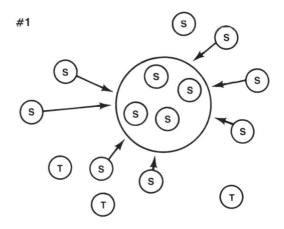

participation flow than the first two illustrations. On pages 84 and 85 are the diagrams of what took place.

Could this teaching team accomplish its written learning objectives, based on the information you have been given? If you don't think so, what could the teachers have done to actually accomplish the objectives? Do you feel this session plan was worked out carefully? Do you think it is realistic?

Much, much more could be written about teaching activities. This chapter has only introduced the subject. In order to make the classroom an exciting experience, a variety of teaching activities need to be used on a fairly regular basis. Children and youth do not often resist new and different ways of teaching, but adults sometimes do. Nevertheless, teachers of adults also need to use different methods. It is wise to "test the waters" carefully in an effort to determine what will work as well as what will not. Above all, don't be afraid to try.

Team teachers have an advantage not enjoyed by the single teacher. One member of a team can take a Sunday off once in a while for the purpose of observing a certain teaching activity in another class. One of the best ways to gain confidence about new methods is to observe someone else in a "live" setting. Observing another teacher (or team of teachers) allows you to decide if you feel comfortable with the teaching activity before you use it yourself. You can also decide how you want to revise or change it to suit your situation.

Notes

1. Donald L. Griggs, *Teaching Teachers to Teach* (Nashville: Abingdon, 1980). Copyright 1974 by Griggs Educational Service.

2. Martha M. Leypoldt, *40 Ways to Teach in Groups* (Valley Forge, Pa.: Judson, 1967), p.17.

Chapter 5

Some Important Questions

This chapter deals with the subject of teacher growth and some other concerns that beginning teachers have. It does not represent an exhaustive treatment of the subject, but rather highlights various aspects of it for new teachers. This chapter answers eight questions:

1. How can I grow as a teacher?
2. What about home visitation?
3. Should I use out-of-class assignments?
4. How can I use questions?
5. What about teaching contracts?
6. What about learning contracts?
7. How long should I teach?
8. Can a teacher *not* teach?

Few persons indeed are born with all the natural skills and abilities needed to be an effective teacher. For most, the road to effectiveness has been paved with workshops, training opportunities, and self-study. Teachers are made, not born. Even in a lifetime of teaching, we will never be perfect teachers or lead perfect sessions. I have never met a perfect teacher, and you probably haven't, either. Wise teachers know that learning is a lifelong process, both for the student and the teacher.

If you are considering teaching or have already agreed to teach, the primary consideration is motivation. Do you really want to teach? Are you willing to do whatever it takes to be an effective teacher, including careful planning and preparation? Are you willing to pursue personal growth and skill development? If you answered yes to these questions, you are ready to take a serious look at possibilities for teacher growth.

Over an extended period of time, the best sessions you teach will be those you have planned carefully. Your best growth experiences will emerge from careful planning as well.

Earlier in this book, the various roles of the teacher were presented. As you begin to consider personal growth, you might want to reflect on these roles and any implications they have for you in your role as a teacher. What does a teacher consider and do? The following points were taken from a little booklet entitled *Me, a Teacher,* which introduces the teaching ministry of the church. As you read the statements, consider the personal growth and skill development implications contained in each. One section of the booklet describes the teacher as follows:

"A *teacher* isn't a Bible expert, *but* has professional help and guidance." One way to grow is to seek advice, suggestions, and ideas from others who have been teaching a while. Look to others in the teaching ministry as resource persons for you, the new teacher.

"A *teacher* doesn't know all the answers, *but* is a learner among learners." If being a learner doesn't threaten you, you're already on your way to teacher growth and development. Don't be embarrassed if some morning you don't know one of the answers. At that moment, a great opportunity for learning is presented to both the teacher and the student, namely, "Let's learn together."

"A *teacher* isn't tied to a rigid program, *but* is free to be creative and flexible." A teacher doesn't need to feel that he or she must be able to do everything there is to do in teaching. You are free to develop those skills and abilities that will prove to be most helpful in your overall development as a teacher. If your session calls for a particular resource or skill that you don't have, feel free to enlist another person to work with you.

"A *teacher* doesn't teach a curriculum, *but* teaches persons." Your students will be persons with needs, problems, strengths, hopes, and dreams. The teacher, not the curriculum, is the key to successful learning. Effectively translating printed materials into the lives of students means effective learning. God works through you, the teacher, as a person who reveals love and truth.

"A *teacher* doesn't teach all the time, *but* takes time to listen." The development of communication skills, i.e., listening and observing, may be the most important place for a new teacher to begin. For some of your students—children, youth, or adults—your class may be the only place they can ever talk with someone who listens and really cares. The impact of the church school will increase when teachers learn to develop finely tuned listening skills.

"A *teacher* doesn't do it alone, *but* is part of a team." When teachers learn together, team effectiveness is increased. Therefore, don't miss an opportunity to learn with other members of your teaching team, or if you're teaching alone, with other teachers in your church school. Your church's life together is based on teamwork. Teamwork in your classroom is important as well.

Types of Teacher Education

There is a wide variety of teacher education events you may want to consider. Some of them are briefly described here. If you wish to pursue these events or others that are not mentioned but don't know where to get information about them, check with the superintendent or chairperson of your board of Christian education.

1. Teachers' meetings. Regular teachers' meetings are expected and scheduled in many churches. A regular feature should be teacher training.

2. Private study. A wealth of resources is available for individual study at home.

3. Team study. Members of a teaching team may select resources for study on a regular basis.

4. Age-level study. Teachers who are teaching the same age level can get together for age-level study, review of resources, discussion of teaching activities, or whatever. If your church school is very small, you can pursue this type of study with teachers from other churches.

5. Cluster of churches. A cluster of churches may bring teachers together for a workshop or training session.

6. One-day training events. Many clusters of churches, associations, or area groupings offer one-day training events that provide a wide variety of training options for teachers.

7. Teacher observation. One of the best ways to learn is to observe another teacher in a live classroom situation. If you are a member of a teaching team, arrangements can be made for you to be absent on a Sunday for the purpose of observation. Discuss with your superintendent the possibility of observing teachers in your church school. If such an opportunity does not exist, ask the superintendent to inquire about the possibility of your observing in another school nearby. A point to remember here is that you want to observe an *effective* teacher, not just any teacher.

8. Community college or evening school courses. More than ever before, community colleges and adult evening schools are offering courses designed for teachers in the church school. If they are not offered in your area and you are interested in this type of training, ask your board of Christian education to request that an educational agency in your area offer such courses.

9. Laboratory training. Training events lasting a week or more are often offered at educational centers, at denominational training centers, or through joint denominational efforts. These are intensive training events that thoroughly explore the subject of teaching. Most also offer intensive age-level study.

10. The media. More and more teaching aids in the media field are becoming available, including closed circuit or community television, video cassettes, videotape, and so forth. Skill development for new teachers includes becoming familiar with new teaching tools as they are developed.

11. Regional denominational office. Most regional offices of your denomination are involved in some type of teacher and leader training. If a certain kind of training interests you (and your board), request information on events that are currently being offered as well as any that might become available in the future.

This is but a brief look at some types of teacher education events and training possibilities. Not every one will be available to every local church; however, some of them will be available, and the beginning teacher needs to determine how much and what type of training to get.

What about Home Visitation?

Most teachers recognize the value of home contact. Yet many teachers experience difficulty in making home contacts for several reasons, including lack of time, lack of organization, and lack of confidence.

Many of the teachers in our church schools, male and female, are employed full-time outside of their homes. Work responsibilities, plus a variety of other commitments, make it difficult for teachers to find time to prepare to teach and to visit students' homes as well. Yet the value of a teacher's presence in the student's home cannot be overestimated.

Home visitation generates many benefits, such as

• basic information about the student, the home environment, and the family unit;

• a mutual review of teacher and student expectations;

• encouragement for the student and the family unit, saying that "you are important";

• an opportunity to use communication skills, especially listening and observing, in a setting outside the classroom;

• an opportunity to secure support for the student's participation in the church school;

• sharing plans, hopes, and dreams;

• an opportunity to discuss and secure commitments;

• an opportunity to express caring for both the student and the student's family;

• an opportunity to share parts of God's story;

• two-way communication—the student often expresses feelings and attitudes more willingly on his or her "home turf" than in the classroom;

• strengthened relationships;

• praying together.

The lack of a consistent approach to home visitation is another reason why some teachers do not visit. A plan for visitation needs to be created by the teacher or the teaching team. Experimentation may be needed to discover the most effective way to make home contacts.

Whether new or experienced, some teachers are unsure of themselves in making home contacts. One of the best ways to gain confidence in home visitation is to visit as a team. A team teacher, a class member, a spouse, or a departmental superintendent could accompany a teacher to provide support and assistance. After a period of time, most teachers are able to gain the confidence necessary to make home contacts alone. However, it is acceptable to continue making home contacts in the company of another person.

Although there is no set of rules for making home contacts, there are some general guidelines. Home contacts should be made when

• teacher and class come together for the first time (if all homes cannot be visited, contact should be made first with families whom the teacher has not met),
• there is a crisis in the life of the student or family unit,
• there have been extended absences due to illness, injury, or other unusual reasons,
• unexplained absences continue after the third consecutive Sunday (A phone call to a student who misses two consecutive Sundays is advisable; a visit should be paid to the home of a student who misses a third consecutive Sunday. Studies of both church and church school dropouts indicate that those persons who are not personally contacted after three absences are usually lost forever to the group. This is especially true of church schools.),
• unusual behaviors in class suggest that the student has a problem. Some of these behaviors include questionable actions, feelings, attitudes, or anger.

Under certain circumstances, the telephone can substitute for home visits. The phone permits a type of two-way communication to take place. However, when continued absences, health problems, crises, or strained relationships and attitudes are involved, the personal visit is a "must."

The length of a home visit is generally determined by the circumstances. A general guide is to keep all visits under thirty minutes. A teacher may find it easy to stay too long. If the purpose of your home contact is teacher-student home relationships, then thirty minutes is sufficient. The very fact that a teacher visits is probably the most significant result of the home contact.

Does the teacher need to do all of the home visitation? No. Others can become involved in the visitation process.

1. All members of the teaching team (if possible) should be involved in making home contacts. Thus the burden of home visitation is shared, and, in most cases, visitation won't fall entirely to any one member of the teaching team.

2. Students—children, youth, and adults—can become involved in making home contacts. Caring and sharing take place when students visit the homes of other class members.

3. Several churches have experienced success through involving other church boards and committees to visit dropouts. For instance, the diaconate can be responsible for contacting persons who have dropped out of the church school. One of the tasks of the diaconate is to express concern and to demonstrate a caring response to all persons who may have become disenchanted or disappointed with any phase of the life of a local congregation. This concern and sharing may also include the ministry of the church school. By teaming with the board of Christian education and its teachers, a total church concern can be expressed for those who are absent, without regard for the reason. Having other persons make contact with students and families may result in securing feedback that the teacher finds helpful.

In summary, each teacher will have to decide how much home contact to make in light of individual circumstances. Home contact is one of the most important aspects of teaching; yet it is often placed on the "back burner" because other responsibilities demand so much of the teacher's time.

Should I Give Out-Of-Class Assignments?

Homework by any other name is still homework. Ask any student! Whether it is called an assignment, an outside assignment, out-of-class work, extra work, or homework, the task sounds the same. Youth and adults, in particular, often have negative feelings toward homework. My grandmother used to tell me when I was a boy that I "could catch more flies with honey than vinegar." At first I wasn't sure what she meant. But eventually the idea began to sink in. Perhaps teachers need to take this saying to heart when it comes to outside work for their students.

Should students be given homework or outside assignments? The answer to this question depends a great deal on the curriculum being taught and the learning objectives used as a basis for the sessions. Some teachers are able to get "extra mileage" out of each session because they have learned the secret of making things happen outside the classroom. Teaching and learning are not restricted to fifty minutes or an hour on Sunday morning. Some of the greatest learning can occur outside the classroom. Togetherness teaching, depending on when it may occur, may have the appearance of an outside assignment.

What is the secret of student participation in activities outside the classroom? Probably the most successful method is for teacher and students to reach an agreement that some teaching/learning will take place outside the classroom. The best time to discuss this is at the beginning of a unit. Teaching activities can be labeled as those that take place inside or outside of the classroom. Over a period of time, a teacher may be able to help students develop an interest in teaching activities that can take place anytime during the week. Sow the seeds carefully. Never make such an assignment without discussing it thoroughly with the students in advance. Secure agreement and commitment, if possible. Sometimes, if properly challenged, students will volunteer to do extra work. Not every student will do this, but be alert to opportunities for highly motivated students to become involved.

Possibilities exist for every student to do some outside work. This includes children, youth, and adults. Some resistance may be expected, probably more from adults than others. However, with proper motivation and encouragement, even adults will invest in learning or class-related activities outside of the classroom.

Outside assignments that seem threatening to the student will fail. A win-lose situation—if you do it, you're a good student; if you don't, you're bad—will be threatening to some students. Encouragement and motivation should be provided at every point. No threats!

Assignments may be given as agreed at any time during the course of a session. Outside teaching/learning activities can emerge from opening activities, any teaching activity, or the closing activity. Whatever is best for the class in the session setting is appropriate.

How Can I Use Questions?

Some teachers are able to ask questions that cause students to think, to probe, and to stretch their minds. Other teachers ask threatening questions to which students don't know the answers. Undoubtedly, skillful questioning can be one of the most effective ways to guide a class in its thinking and learning.

Questions don't require a lot of research, are ready for use without extra or intensive work, and can be used in every teaching activity or setting. The proper use of questions in home and family contacts can provide the teacher with valuable insights into students' needs. Most teachers use many questions in every session.

On the other hand, questions can also be a liability. Compare their positive and negative implications. Questions can be

- a help or a hindrance,
- nonthreatening or threatening,
- helpful or hurtful,
- simple or difficult,
- clear or unclear,
- fun or boring,
- affirming or embarrassing to the learner.

In considering which question to use, the key question is, Why am I asking the question? Questions asked "on the spur of the moment" often place the teacher or student (or both) in an awkward or difficult position. The wise use of questions calls for the teacher to think through in advance questions to use in teaching activities or as linking pieces in other activities.

Questions fall into four general categories. As you become more experienced in teaching, you may want to check out other discussions of questions, some of which will be much more detailed than this one.

1. Content recall. This category suggests that the student should remember something in order to answer the question. Recall could include content, experiences, feelings, attitudes, or values. One of the problems with this type of question is that by asking it, the teacher is suggesting that there is a right answer. These types of questions are much akin to taking a test, and "if I don't know the answers, I fail or get a bad grade." When a teacher asks a student a content recall question, there is always a risk that the student will not know the answer and be hurt by the experience. Some students have dropped out of church school because of such an experience.

The teacher who asks content recall questions should watch for clues from those who think they know the answers. Among children, the upraised hand, facial expressions, or body language tell the teacher that they think they know the answer. If a student volunteers under these circumstances and the answer is wrong, it is usually not a negative experience.

2. Feeling questions. These questions deal with feelings, values, attitudes, climate, sensitivities, and nonverbal expressions. It is appropriate to ask questions that deal with feelings. To ignore feelings or attitudes in an individual or in the class that need to be brought into the open will not help learning take place; in fact, feelings may become a barrier to learning. If a teacher senses strong feelings in a statement or expression of some type—nonverbal or verbal—questions of concern are appropriate. In most cases, it is best to begin questions something like this:

"I'm not sure how you really feel about it . . . can you help me know how you feel?"

"I'm not sure I understand what you are saying . . . do I hear you saying that . . . ?"

"Do I sense that you feel . . . ?"

"Do you feel that . . . ?"

"Do I hear you saying that . . . ?"

It is usually very helpful for the person who has made a statement that expresses strong feeling to rephrase the statement. The teacher can help the student. Often the restatement will provide the person with an opportunity to think through clearly just what he or she meant by the statement or expression.

3. Reflective questions. These questions direct the student back into him- or herself to examine the issue or subject. Questions of this type provide an opportunity for the student to dig deeper into self, to examine real meanings, and to stretch his or her own mind. Locke E. Bowman states that "once a student has responded to a given question, the teacher should ask him/herself: Is there more on this student's mind? Has this student something to share? How can I reach for it? This is where the teacher senses the need to probe, to ask other questions, to dig for more 'gold' that is to be mined from students' insights. Why? Why is one of the key probing questions."[2]

Bowman offers another piece of advice: "Many questions that begin 'Is . . . ?' and 'Are . . . ?' can only be answered with a yes or no. They are *not* very productive, so they should be followed with 'Why?' or 'Why do you think so?'"[3]

Reflective questions may be addressed to individual students or to the whole class. In whatever way they are used, if asked correctly, they will usually guide the individual or class into the subject for more in-depth thinking.

4. Enabling questions. Since the teacher is an enabler, an appropriate way to help students is to provide guidance and advice through questions rather than by "giving orders." An example of an enabling question is, Would it be helpful to you if . . . ?

The very fact you are asking the question indicates that you probably think it would be helpful if the student did whatever is in question. However, asking this type of question throws the decision making onto the student. The student may choose not to do it and, if so, has made a decision. Most students will sooner or later see the wisdom of the enabling suggestion. They will also recognize that the teacher gave them an option rather than telling them what to do. (Such questions are not appropriate in emergencies or other types of crisis situations, such as a fire or an accident.)

Questions can be asked of and by many persons. Teachers can address questions to individual students as well as to the whole class. Students can ask questions of each other or of the teacher. Questions can be used in research and assignments. They can be sent home to be asked of parents, friends, neighbors, brothers, and sisters. Questions can be used in instructions, tests, and a wide variety of teaching activities.

What about Teaching Contracts?

The term "teaching contract" or "teaching agreement" may be new to you, since not every church uses them in teacher recruitment. (If the word "contract" is too formal for your church school, the term "agreement" may be substituted.) There are some distinct advantages to making contracts or agreements, both for the teacher and the board of Christian education. One of them is that teacher expectations are clearly identified.

Note the following characteristics of a good teacher contract:

1. The church's expectations are clearly set forth.

2. The teacher and the church are committed to an agreed-upon time period to teach.

3. Requirements for training and skill development are stated.

4. Support systems are clarified.

5. Relationships are clarified.

6. Evaluation is not assumed but is stated as an expectation.

The teaching contract includes five major components:

1. The parties involved are identified. Usually these are the teacher and the recruiting group, such as a board of Christian education, a committee on Christian education, superintendents, or others.

2. An agreed-upon period of time is stated. It might range from teaching a six-week short course through several years. Most teachers and boards like the one-year contract since it seems to be neither too short nor too long.

3. Expectations about training are usually identified. For instance, a board of Christian education may expect its teachers to be

involved in at least one (or more) training experience during the course of the year.

4. Often a review process is suggested or is actually spelled out in the contract. This is agreed upon in advance by the teacher as well as by the contracting group.

5. The age level that the teacher will teach should be specified.

What about Learning Contracts?

Some church school teachers are making use of learning contracts. A learning contract is an agreement between the student and the teacher. The agreement may cover a wide range of learning possibilities, including subjects for study, research, projects, testing, writing, participation, and others. The key element in a learning contract is that both teacher and student know what has been agreed upon, including the time framework within which the work is to be accomplished.

Learning contracts (you may prefer the term "learning agreements") may be written between a teacher and a student or between a teacher and the class. They are used for the benefit of the learner as well as the teacher. A learning agreement calls for a degree of commitment and maturity from the student. In order for a student to write a learning contract, he or she needs some awareness or knowledge of what can be done. In other words, the student needs to have a general idea of what he or she is attempting to do as well as to be aware of the options that are available for completing the agreement.

It is not necessary to use learning contracts for every unit or every semester of work. However, from time to time, depending on the students' interest and motivation, a learning contract with one or more students may be an effective way for learning to take place. The use of learning centers, as well as decentralized learning experiences, encourages the use of learning contracts. It is also possible to develop commitments in learning contracts that include persons other than teacher and student. Other persons to involve in learning contracts are parents, brothers and sisters, school friends, class members, and others.

An example of a teaching contract (or teaching agreement):

TEACHING CONTRACT
for

_____ and the Board of Christian Education of
(name)

_____ .
(church)

_____ accepts the invitation of the Board of
(name)

Christian Education to serve as a school teacher in our church's
educational ministry from _____ to _____ .
month/year   month/year

You, the teacher, may expect from the Board of Christian Education:
- support and encouragement
- worship, study, and growth experiences
- training sessions
- guidance and suggestions/directions
- recognition of your work
- resources, materials, and supplies.
- a listening ear to your ideas
- caring

The Board of Christian Education expects from the teacher:
- growth and development (personal)
- involvement in the life of the church
- help given to students to learn and develop
- preparation for teaching responsibilities
- cooperation with other teachers
- participation in training opportunities
- regular attendance and early arrival
- presence at teacher planning meetings

We join hands with God and this congregation to work toward the
goals of the educational ministry of this church.

_____   _____
(Teacher's signature)   (Signature, chairperson of
                                 Board of Christian Education)

_____   _____
(Church moderator)   (Pastor)

LEARNING CONTRACT (AGREEMENT)

_____ plans to study the following sub-
(Student's name)   ject(s): (or complete a project, or
                                        whatever is appropriate).

I will use the following steps: (These might include the use of learning
                                 centers, books to be read, project steps
                                 to be done, dialogue or conversations to
                                 take place, etc.)

1.

2.

3.

4.

5.

6.

I plan to share the results of my work with my teacher and/or class by

_____
            (date)

I plan to complete all of my study/work by _____ .
                                                      (date)

_____
(Student's name, or class name, or title)

_____
(Teacher's name)

_____
(Parent's name, if it applies)

How Long Should I Teach?

This book will probably be read by new teachers or by persons who have never taught. To these readers the question posed in the subheading may seem inappropriate. But experience suggests that, with time, volunteer teachers get tired, bored, worn out, frustrated, or overextended. If and when that happens, it is quite proper to seek relief from teaching, even temporarily. Many teachers benefit from a three-month "vacation" during the course of teaching for a year or two.

If you, even in your first few years of teaching, begin to experience some of the feelings described above, discuss them with a member of your teaching team. Seek advice from the superintendent or a member of the board of Christian education. If your feelings about teaching are not strongly positive or if you really do not have the time to prepare properly for teaching, you will probably communicate some of your frustration to the class. As a result, you will not be able to offer the best teaching/learning experiences to your students, and your tension will increase. When this happens (and sometimes the teacher can go quite a period of time without an awareness of such feelings, the teacher needs to "stop everything," at least temporarily, and take stock of the situation creeping up on you by carefully assessing your feelings, as described in chapter 1.

Some teachers find it refreshing to teach different age levels. For instance, after several years of teaching children, some teachers benefit from switching to teens or adults. The opposite can be true too. A change in room setting, age level, or teaching team often provides relief. Above all, when you are tired of teaching, be sure to talk with someone about it. It may be better to drop out or change something at that point than to continue to teach under stress or dissatisfaction.

Can a Teacher *Not* Teach?

Teaching, regardless of its quality, goes on all the time a teacher and a class are together. There is no time during a session that a teacher can decide *not* to teach. The teacher teaches by what he or she says or does not say. The teacher teaches by what he or she does and does not do.

A number of years ago, James Ashbrook discussed this in a booklet entitled *The Pastor as Teacher-Learner: A Dialogue.* He asserts that "we cannot not teach. People read us without realizing it. We instruct them without knowing it. They are learning from us all the time."

We teach by what we do and how we do it as much as by what we say. People learn what matters to us from our behavior and our attitudes. This unintended "lesson" is taught more in what we unexpectedly "give off" than in what we consciously "intend."

When I ask someone how she is without listening to her answer, she learns that I go through motions without always meaning them. When I ask someone how he is and wait for him to respond, he is learning that I care about him.[4]

The old saying, Practice what you preach, is easily translated into teaching. We can change it to say, Practice what you teach. If you always demonstrate what you say you believe, teaching will always take place. Your students will understand you well if they find that your teaching and doing are consistent. In a *Baptist Leader* article, Glee Yoder tells the delightful story of two children who demonstrate what teaching is all about:

While his mother was shopping in a supermarket, a small boy began playing train with the glass baby food jars on the shelf. One by one he would take the jars off the shelf and line them up "train-fashion" on the floor. A clerk, seeing his play, told him to put the jars back. Rounding the corner of the stack, the clerk again heard the tinkle of glass. Angry this time, he shouted, "Stop that! Put those jars back on the shelf. You'll break them!"

But before long, the clerk heard the familiar sound. Hurrying to the area, he saw the boy with another boy, not much larger, kneeling down beside the little "pretender" with his arm around him. As the newcomer placed a jar on the shelf, the other boy put one on the shelf. This went on until all the jars had been placed in the proper spot. The clerk approached the two and asked. "How did you get him to put those jars back?" Looking up with a smile on his face, the other boy replied, "He doesn't understand when you talk to him that way. He understands what I say because I love it into him!"[5]

This is great teaching! Remember, you cannot *not* teach!

Conclusion

Teaching is about "growing"—about students who will grow and develop as persons and in their faith, and about teachers who will mature in their faith, skill, and overall teaching ability. A guide from Scripture is found in 2 Timothy 2:15: "Do your best to present yourself to God as one approved by him, a workman who has no need to be ashamed, rightly explaining the word of truth."

Teachers and students learn together. I would like to close this chapter with a statement made by Vernon Law: "When you're through learning, you're through."

May yours be a lifetime of learning—a long one!

Notes

1. This material is adapted from the booklet *Me, A Teacher?* written by Mrs. Donna Mason, director of Christian education at Fremont Presbyterian Church in Sacramento, California.

2. Locke E. Bowman Jr., *Seventy Cues for Teachers* (Scottsdale, Ar.: The Arizona Experiment, 1972).

3. Ibid.

4. James B. Ashbrook, *The Pastor as Teacher-Learner: A Dialogue* (Valley Forge, Pa.: American Baptist Convention, 1967), p. 7.

5. Glee Yoder, "Happiness Is . . . a Church School Teacher," *Baptist Leader* 41, no. 10 (January 1980): 9. Used by permission of American Baptist Board of Education and Publication.

Leader's Guide:
Basic Teacher Skills

The five chapters of this book provide the basis for five learning experiences for new teachers under the guidance and leadership of a trained instructor, experienced teacher, or pastor. Two hours of class time are needed to address the content of each chapter effectively. New and potential teachers need a minimum of ten hours of training to prepare them to serve as volunteer teachers in the church school.

Five two-hour sessions spread over a five-week period are ideal for teaching the course. If this is not possible, select a format that matches schedules and interests. A ten-week course during the church school hour on Sunday morning is another model to consider. It calls for no extra meetings for busy persons. But be sure you provide sixty minutes of teaching, even if this requires an earlier starting time.

A third model to consider provides two sessions of four hours each on two consecutive or two alternating Saturdays. The final two-hour session could be offered a week later on a weekday evening. Still another model could be built around three-hour sessions offered on three consecutive or three alternating Sundays. A concluding session to complete a ten-hour course could be provided on a weekday evening.

The makeup of your group will somewhat determine the activities and subjects you will offer. If your group is composed only of persons who have never taught, then you will want to select the most basic exercises and experiences. If your group includes persons who have never taught and some who are teaching, you may want to select a different mix of activities so that the more experienced teachers will feel they are being helped as well. You may find that you need to devote more than the suggested time to some activities and not as much time to others in the session outlines that follow.

Whenever possible, you should model teacher roles, styles, activities, and skills for your participants in everything you do. Observing an effective teacher or leader is a valuable way to learn. Use newsprint, chalkboards, dialogue, small groups, audiovisual equipment, etc. Involve students with the newsprint or chalkboard. Teach them how to use the equipment you use in your sessions. Involve students at every stage of teaching. Learning by doing is another valuable way to learn that can be demonstrated in these sessions.

Here are some expectations to keep in mind for the group that you will teach. Encourage the sponsoring group to assist you in fulfilling these expectations.

1. Seek agreement on the number of sessions to be taught and the length of each session.

2. When recruiting participants, the sponsoring group will raise the expectation that participants should attend all sessions.

3. Each participant should have his or her own copy of the text.

4. If possible, participants should have completed reading chapter 1 prior to the first session of the course.

5. Some between-class assignments and reading will be expected from participants. The overall objectives for this teacher training course may be summarized as follows.

By the end of this course, each participant will

• be able to identify basic teacher roles,

• discover personal strengths and skills through personal assessment, as well as future personal growth and skill development possibilities,

• be able to plan a session,

- experience three different teaching methods and be able to identify and use each method,
- be able to begin to make plans for personal teacher growth and skill development.

Keep these course objectives before you as you plan each session for your class or group.

Session 1: The Challenge of Teaching and What You Bring to It (Chapter 1)

Before you make your session plans, familiarize yourself with the content of chapter 1. Read it through several times. Be sure to make a brief outline for your use as you plan.

The session will be easier for you to plan if you break the two-hour session into one-hour segments and take a fifteen-minute break between the two segments.

Session 1 Objectives

1. By the end of the first hour, each participant will know the first names of class members and will have discovered some history and background of several of them.

2. By the end of this session, each participant will be committed to the course objectives.

3. By the end of this session, each participant will have recorded some things that deal with his or her relationship to God and to God's story.

The First Hour

Wear a name tag and provide name tags for all participants to wear.

1. Get Acquainted (20 minutes)

Even if the teachers are already acquainted, there are many new things they can learn about each other. It might be fun, as well as educational, to share some of their early experiences with the church schools they attended. Ask them to share such things as *(a)* their age when they first attended a church school; *(b)* what church school they attended; *(c)* who took them or how they got started;

(d) the best thing they can remember about their church school experiences; *(e)* a teacher they liked and why.

If the group numbers fewer than seven persons, this sharing can be done in the total group. If the group numbers seven or more persons, the sharing should be done in pairs. Bring them back to the total group to share one or two interesting things they have learned about each other. Ask them to introduce each other to the total group.

Another way to begin this session would be to talk about favorite church school teachers. Which teacher is remembered most vividly? Why? If someone is present who never attended a church school, ask him or her to tell about a favorite public school teacher.

2. *Check Out Expectations* (15 minutes)

Give each participant a three-by-five-inch card or some plain paper. Ask all of them to write down in brief what they hope to receive from this course. Encourage them to share their expectations about what they hope to receive from the instruction. Also ask them to write down any questions, doubts, or fears they have about becoming teachers. After they have completed their writing, ask each person to share briefly one or two items with the total class.

Using newsprint or chalkboard, share the stated course objectives found in the opening section of the leader's guide. Answer any questions they may have about course objectives. Check with the group to see if they are ready to move into the basic course material.

3. *Partnership with God* (25 minutes)

Ask participants to turn with you to this page of the leader's guide. Now complete the exercise "Partnership with God" (below). After they have made their lists, form pairs and ask each participant to share with a partner what each has written about his or her experiences of teaming with God in other phases of life.

Exercise: Partnership with God

As you look back over your life, what other partnerships with God can you recall? The teaching partnership may be new to you, but it will most likely not be your first experience of teaming with God. List some other experiences in your Christian life when you covenanted with God to accomplish or receive something.

(Examples: prayed for someone's healing, asked God to join with you in raising your child, pleaded with God to bring peace into the world, volunteered to do some aspect of God's work, etc.)

a. _____

b. _____

c. _____

d. _____

Break (10-15 minutes)
The Second Hour

In recent training sessions for new teachers that I have led, some of the participants had attended church school all their lives, while others had become Christians later in life or were of a different faith tradition and had no background in church school or the Bible. The following exercise is basic for all new teachers, regardless of background or experience.

4. God's Story and My Story (20 minutes)

Ask your students to turn to this page and fill out the three sections below. This step is a pause in order to take inventory. It is important for participants to identify what they think is most significant in God's story and how it has affected their lives. Ask them to fill out sections A, B, and C individually. When they have completed that task, they should form new pairs to share with each other what they have written about God's story.

Exercise: God's Story and My Story

A. What I Know about God's Story

List the five most significant facts (content) that you know about God's story.

1._____

2._____

3._____

4._____

5._____

B. What God's Story Has Done to/for/with Me

List at least three important ways in which God's story has affected your life and lifestyle.

1._____
2._____
3._____

C. My Feelings about God's Story

Persons who have committed their lives to telling God's story have definite feelings about it. Describe some of your feelings about the story and its impact on your life.

5. *Sowing Seeds* (20 minutes)

Ask your group to begin the exercise below. Have them write down one or two significant seeds they have planted and list the results of their planting. After a few minutes of work on the exercise, bring them together into the total group and ask several of them to share briefly an illustration of a seed sown and a result that came from the sowing. On newsprint or a chalkboard, draw two columns: "The Seed" and "The Result." Ask each person who shares to come to the newsprint or chalkboard and write one item in each column. Help each have the experience of writing and talking in front of the group. Each person who participates should share briefly an account of what happened. This provides him or her with an opportunity to share verbally in front of the total group. Keep the exercise moving along—no sermons! Ask them to do further work on this exercise at home.

Exercise: Sowing Seeds

A farmer friend once explained to me what potatoes need to grow big. I followed his instructions, and in the first hill of potatoes dug late that summer I found the biggest potato I've ever grown—the size of a football! It's easy to remember that particular planting and the results.

Make a list of some seeds you've planted in the lives of other people and what happened as a result. Each of you has already had some experiences in life as a "sower." What happened? Include your family, friends, neighbors, church friends, coworkers, strangers, folks you grew up with, etc., as part of your garden.

The Seed	The Results

6. The Challenge of the Learner (15 minutes)

Each teacher has a challenge to respond to the needs of each student and to his or her potential to grow. The needs can range all the way from deep personal concerns, the need to become a Christian, and a host of everyday problems to the need for fellowship and fun or the need to be touched by one who cares and loves. Good teaching responds to the needs of persons. Help them understand that the variety of needs of the students in the class provides great opportunities for decision making, growth, and development to take place.

If your class is composed only of teachers who are not currently teaching and have never taught, use exercise A. If you have a mix of teachers who have never taught and some who are now teaching, assign the former to exercise A and the latter to exercise B. After about five minutes of individual work ask them to share their list of challenges in group A and group B, using only one word or phrase for each contribution to the group.

Exercise: The Challenge of the Learner

A. If you are not yet teaching, select the age group you would like to teach. Include no names, but make a list of the general needs and problems that might be expected in this group that could present a real challenge to you. List a possible response for each if you can.

Challenge	Response

B. If you are already teaching, complete this part of the exercise. List the needs and challenges you observe in your class. Do this by listing the person's first name, the need or challenge, and a possible response.

Name	Challenge	Response

7. Summarize (5 minutes)

Briefly summarize what you feel is the most significant point in this session. Place a piece of newsprint near the door and ask the participants to write a feeling word on the paper as they leave. The word should describe how they feel about the first session. Give the assignment to read chapter 2. Assign any other of the additional exercises that follow that you feel would be important for their learning.

Session 2: Sorting Out the Pieces of the Teaching Puzzle (Chapter 2)

Be sure to read chapter 2 several times so that you are thoroughly familiar with its content. Think about what you heard and observed in your first session with the group. As you consider the contents of chapter 2, think about what parts will have the greatest meaning and provide the most help to this group of potential teachers.

Session 2 Objectives

1. That each class member will be able to identify seven basic teacher roles and assess his or her skill in each role;

2. That each participant will experience at least one exercise dealing with communication skills;

3. That each student will decide which methods of learning are best for him or her;

4. That each participant will be able to use togetherness teaching when the opportunity presents itself.

The First Hour

What is the best way to bring participants on board? What opening activity could you use that would bring the group together and also illustrate a teaching activity they could use? One suggestion is given here; however, you may want to select another that better meets the needs of your class.

1. Beginning the Session (15 minutes)

Bring out the newsprint on which the participants recorded feeling words at the close of session 1. Describe your feelings about session 1. Ask participants if their feelings have changed since the last session. If so, how? Conclude this section with a brief overview of chapter 2, highlighting several of the main points.

Other options for beginning this session include
- a review of last week's session,
- a short communications exercise (selected from exercises in this leader's guide or from other sources of your own choosing),
- a brief devotional, Bible study, singing, or some combination thereof.

At the conclusion of your opening activity, pause for a moment or two of prayer. Point out to your group that prayer is appropriate at any point during a session.

2. Basic Teacher Roles (20 minutes)

It is important that every new teacher have a general understanding of the various roles played by a volunteer teacher in the church school. It is equally important that each beginning teacher be aware of his or her own degree of skill or ability related to each role.

On newsprint or a chalkboard write a one-sentence description of each of the basic teacher roles summarized on page 26. Some class members will have completed the exercise on page 27; some will not. Take a few minutes to allow those who have not completed the exercise to do so. Then divide the class into small groups of two or three persons to discuss their self-analysis and personal feelings about teacher roles. At the conclusion of the discussion deal with unanswered questions from the class.

3. Different Ways to Learn (25 minutes)

The "teacher, student, content" diagram found on page 28 contains one of the most important concepts in the book. Reproduce the diagram on newsprint and make a five-minute presentation to the class as to why you think it is so very important.

Conclude your brief presentation by focusing on the importance of student learning. Learning may take place in many ways. Some ways to learn may be right for one group but less effective for another.

Ask participants to complete the exercise on page 29 if they have not already done so. Divide them into pairs to share their answers to the first two steps of this exercise. Then reassemble the total group to list on newsprint or chalkboard those ways to learn that they would eventually like to use with students. Ask each person to go to the newsprint or chalkboard and write his or her items for the group to see.

Break (10-15 minutes)

The Second Hour

4. Dale's Cone of Learning (20 minutes)

It is important for new teachers to understand Dale's simple formula that people remember only 10 percent of what they hear, 50 percent of what they see and hear, and 90 percent of what they do. Ask them to add examples from their own lives and church school experiences to items 1-6 on Dale's Cone of Learning. (The cone is found on page 31.) Do this in small groups of three persons. Ask each group to add items to the six categories and then report to the total group. List all the ideas on newsprint or chalkboard. An extra step you may want to consider is to ask the participants to locate the methods of learning that they want to use in Dale's cone.

5. Communication Skills (20 minutes)

How you prepare your session for delivery and what you expect from it are two important factors of good communication. We tend to take our methods of communication for granted—as on my wife's birthday when I went to buy her a traditional card. However, instead of buying a birthday card for a wife, I somehow managed to get one for a husband (there were identical cards for each spouse side by side) and gave it to my wife. The message was certainly different—and so was her response!

Teachers need to listen for facts and feelings. You can learn to listen with your eyes and your intuition as well as your ears. It would be unreasonable to expect all teachers or students to grasp these skills at the same rate. Do not be surprised if progress is slow. The important thing is to keep trying.

Exercise: Listening for Facts[1]

1. Form clusters of three persons at random, preferably bringing persons together who don't know each other very well.

2. Identify each member of the cluster as person A, B, or C.

Person A will be the "speaker," B will be the "listener," and C will be the "observer."

3. Speaker A is to tell listener B certain facts about himself or herself, such as name, occupation, hobby, and place of birth. B is to respond with factual data that he or she has heard, without additional comment. Observer C is to assure that the feedback is accurate and complete. Take no more than three or four minutes for this process.

4. Once the first cycle is complete, ask B to become the speaker, C the listener, and A the observer. Repeat step 3. Next carry through step 3 with C as speaker, A as listener, and B as observer.

6. *Togetherness Teaching* (15 minutes)

Ask the members of your class if they have any questions about togetherness teaching. Be sure each person understands the meaning of the term. As a total group, field and answer questions from students.

Exercise

Ask each person to turn to the work he or she did in the first hour on page 29. Study the list for a moment. Now mark a *T* next to each circled item that provides the possibility of togetherness teaching. Add other ways to learn to the list, if possible.

In the total group, write all items that received a *T*. Brainstorm a list of possible settings in the church and community that would be suitable for togetherness teaching. This list might include individuals, locations, settings, institutions, classes, etc. By creating a lengthy list of possibilities, you are planting ideas in the minds of new teachers that will eventually take root.

7. *Summarize* (5 minutes)

Summarize session 2 in two minutes. Give participants a preview of session 3 with its focus on learning how to plan a session. Assign chapter 3 as advance reading for the next session. Close with prayer.

Ask the participants to evaluate this session by holding "thumbs up" if they feel great about it, "hands level" if it was OK, and "thumbs down" if it wasn't that helpful. If you received a number of "hands level" votes, what could have been done to improve the session to rate a "thumbs up"? If there were any "thumbs down" votes, think about what happened during the session. What could have been changed or modified in order to improve the learning experience?

Additional Exercise Related to Session 2
Participation Chart

Student participation is very important in teaching. Does each student participate? Do one or two persons dominate? Do you relate to each student? If you can't assess it yourself, recruit others to help you learn about participation in your class.

In charting conversation, place the name of each student and your own in one of the circles. As conversation takes place, mark the direction of the flow with an arrow. Each time conversation takes place, mark it on the line to that person. Return arrows indicate responses. Arrows can go in any direction. On the next page is a sample of what a chart might look like. Use 8½-by-11-inch paper.

After your chart has been completed, study it carefully within the context of the session. Be sure to date the chart and place the theme of the session with the date for future reference.

Ask the following questions:

1. Did each student participate in a meaningful way?
2. Which students did not participate? Why?
3. Was there much interaction among students? If not, why?
4. Do most of the participation lines move from the teacher to the students? Why?
5. What did you learn about the quality of participation? (Note: The number of interactions is not always a true indicator of the depth of participation. A serious student may choose to participate less; but when he or she does, it may be a significant contribution. Quality is as important as quantity.)
6. How do you feel about the participation that you observed in your class?

Keep the charts and refer to them when you do your session planning. There may be some clues for your planning.

It is not necessary to do a participation chart for every session. If you are experiencing problems in persuading students to participate, you will already know about it. Once a month or once every

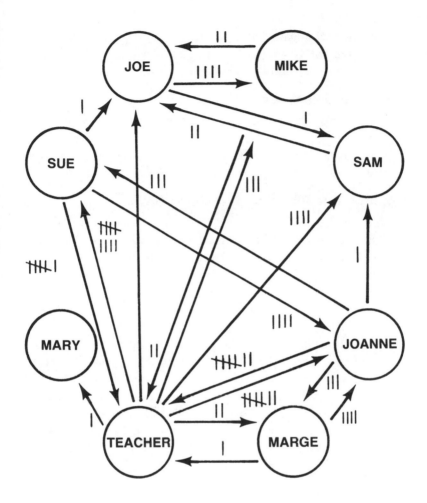

two months may be sufficient until you are fully aware of each person's participation.

Session 3: The Teacher's Dozen—Thirteen Steps in Planning a Session (Chapter 3)

Two different session plans are presented for your consideration in session 3. If you choose the simulation game, be sure to allow enough time to prepare and set up the game. If you use the game, the first hour will be used to play it. The second hour will be used to debrief the game and study several of the planning steps.

Session 3 Objectives

1. That each person experience some of the steps of the planning process.

2. That each person will be able to relate several of the steps in planning to actual planning experiences for teaching.

Option 1: The Planning Simulation Game

Materials needed

Rand-McNally Road Atlas, latest edition (preferably one for each five participants); instruction sheets for all participants (appendix A); four large manila envelopes (9-by-12-inch), each with instructions given in appendix C and with contents as described in appendix B for each team; debriefing handouts for all participants (appendix D).

NOTE: This planning simulation is organized around four basic questions related to taking a trip: (1) Where are we now? (2) Where do we want to go? (3) How are we going to get there? (4) How will we know when we are there? These four questions encompass the session-planning steps in "The Teacher's Dozen" in the following manner: Where are we now? (steps 1-4); Where do we want to go? (steps 5-6); How are we going to get there? (steps 7-12); How will we know when we are there? (step 13).

The First Hour

1. Introduction

The size of your group will determine how you play the game. If the group has ten participants, form two teams of five persons. If the group numbers from six to nine persons, form two teams. If the group numbers five or fewer persons, play the game as one group. If your group numbers eleven or more persons, you may want to form three or more teams. Remember that each team will need an atlas. You may want to ask the host or sponsoring churches to provide several atlases for this game.

The creator of the simulation game is the Reverend Jeffrey D. Jones, pastor of First Baptist Church, Pitman, New Jersey, and editor of *Young Adult Clipboard*, a resource for young-adult ministries. Jeff initially developed the game as a teaching tool to learn how to plan for youth ministries. It has been adapted for use in this book by church school teachers and is used by permission.

Distribute the instruction sheets (appendix A), and read them aloud as participants follow along. Answer any questions that they may have about the directions.

2. The Simulation Game

Distribute an atlas and "Where are we now?" envelopes to each group and tell them to begin. Envelopes *2, 3,* and *4* should be placed in different locations, and the groups will move about as they attempt to locate them. Use other rooms and locations in the building in which you meet. The locations should be different for each group.

3. Debriefing

When the groups have finished, bring them together for a time of reflection and debriefing. There is no scoring system for the game; so there is no winner (or loser!). If a group should ask about this, you can note that the instructions never mention competition between the groups. Their only objective was to complete the game as quickly and as accurately as possible. Follow these steps as you guide the debriefing of the simulation.

a) Deal with feelings.
• How do you feel now?
• What feelings did you have during the simulation?
• What happened to generate those feelings?

b) Deal with learning.
• What did you learn from participating in this? about yourself? about others?

• How does this relate to other involvements and responsibilities you have?

c) Distribute the handout (appendix D) and deal with planning.
• Note the parallel between the simulation and planning.
• Review the relationships as indicated in the handout. When

you reach "How will we know when we are there?" ask groups to share the characteristics they developed.

• Explore the differences and similarities they developed between the simulation and planning.

Break

If some of the first hour remains at the conclusion of the game, move ahead with debriefing. However, at the completion of the first full hour of work, take a break of at least fifteen minutes.

The Second Hour

4. Further Debriefing (15 minutes)

If participants need further debriefing, address their questions or concerns about planning and how it is done.

5. Steps in Planning a Session (20 minutes)

Ask the group to turn to the page of cutout labels in chapter 3. Use scissors to cut out all the labels on the page. As they work at this project, let "small talk" take place, since they will still be buzzing about some of the things that happened in the planning game.

On newsprint or chalkboard, write the thirteen steps in planning a session. Following the suggestions in the note at the beginning of this session, draw large circles around the steps that relate to each of the four questions about taking a trip. Have your students place the labels in four stacks, matching the four questions from the simulation game. Then spread out each stack so that the related session-planning steps for each question are separate from the others. Help them see the relationship between the game and the various session-planning steps. Field questions from the group.

6. Learning Objectives (15 minutes)

Learning objectives fall under the question, Where do we want to go? It's difficult to say that any one of the four planning questions is more important than the others. However, "if you don't know where you're going, it doesn't really matter how you get there."

Ask your students to turn to step 6 in chapter 3. Review the text material, especially emphasizing the illustrations provided there. You might want to prepare several examples of other learning objectives you have used. You can further illustrate learning objectives by showing them the session objectives that you, the teacher, have used at the beginning of each session in the leader's guide. Answer any questions they may have about learning objectives. If time permits, practice writing an objective as a group, using the next session as a background.

7. *Summary-Closure* (10 minutes)

Briefly review the events of session 3. Share with participants several observations from the session that will be encouraging and supportive of the class.

Assign chapter 4 to be read for the next session. Ask each person to bring a set of curriculum materials to session 4. If some participants are not teaching, ask them to secure a set from a superintendent or a member of the board of Christian education for the age level they would like to teach. Give each person a three-by-five-inch card on which to record his or her feelings about the simulation game later in the week. Ask them to bring the cards with them to the next session.

In closing, share one of the six Scripture passages listed on page 4 (chapter 1). Encourage them in their learning and growing; personal growth has particularly significant meaning for the teacher. Join hands in a circle and lead the group in a closing prayer.

Note

1. Adapted from William C. Cline, *Growing As a Caring Community* (Valley Forge: American Baptist National Ministries, 1979) p. 15.

Appendix A

Instructions

You and your group are participating in a survival skills training course. To give you practice in the skills you have been learning, you have been transported from the training site in Chicopee, Massachusetts, to an unknown town. Your task is to travel to an unknown destination. In order to do this, you must obtain and analyze information that is available in several locations around the town you are in. At each location you will find a large envelope with information written on it that will enable you to answer one of the following questions:

- Where are we now?
- Where do we want to go?
- How are we going to get there?
- How will we know when we are there?

Inside each large envelope are six small envelopes, each with a possible answer written on it. When you believe you have answered the question correctly, open the large envelope, select the appropriate small envelope, and open it. The paper inside will tell you whether or not you are correct. If you are correct, you will also be told the location at which you can obtain the information that will enable you to answer the next question.

If you are not correct or if the answer you thought was correct is not written on one of the envelopes, then use the clues to determine which of the given options is the correct one. When you have made your decision, open that envelope. Repeat this process at each location, except for the last, where you will be given other directions.

If at any point you are stumped and cannot decide on an answer, you may open the small envelope attached to the outside back of the large envelope. The paper inside will give you further information that should enable you to reach a decision. Open these only as a last resort.

The atlas will give you additional information that you need to answer the questions. Note especially the index of towns and the mileage indicators along the routes.

Several other groups are also participating in this experience, although the locations at which they receive information are different from yours. Both speed and accuracy will be used to determine your group's success in completing this exercise.

You will be given an hour to complete the game, so plan your time accordingly.

Appendix B: Envelope Contents

Envelope 1

1. Tape the "Where are we now?" instructions and clues (see appendix C) to the outside front of the large envelope.

2. Write or type the following on a three-by-five-inch index card: "You are in Rhode Island. The broken sign said, Rockville—2 miles."

3. Write or type: "Open this if you are stumped" on a small letter-sized envelope; insert the card described above into the envelope, and tape it to the outside back of the large envelope.

4. Prepare six small envelopes as described below and place them inside the large envelope. On the outside of each envelope write or type one of the following towns:

New London, Connecticut
Hanson, Massachusetts
Haverhill, Massachusetts
Georges Mill, New Hampshire
Exeter, Rhode Island
Hope Valley, Rhode Island

In envelopes 1 through 5 insert a piece of paper that says, "Sorry. Try again."

5. In envelope 6 insert a piece of paper that says, "Congratulations! You are right!" Proceed to (location) for further instructions.

Envelope 2

1. Tape the "Where Do We Want to Go?" instructions and clues (see appendix C) to the outside front of the large envelope.

2. Write or type the following on a three-by-five-inch index card: "The destination is in Connecticut. The college is Wesleyan University. The river that forms the valley is the Connecticut River."

3. Write or type "Open this if you are stumped" on a small

envelope; insert the card described above into the envelope, and tape it to the back of the large envelope.

4. Prepare six small letter envelopes as described below and place them inside the large envelope. On the outside of each envelope write or type one of the following towns:

Middletown, Rhode Island
Middletown, Massachusetts
Middleboro, Massachusetts
Central Village, Connecticut
Middle Haddam, Connecticut
Middletown, Connecticut

In envelopes 1 through 5 insert a piece of paper that says, "Sorry. Try again."

5. In envelope 6 insert a piece of paper that says, "Congratulations! You are right! Proceed to (location) for further instructions."

Envelope 3

1. Tape the "How Are We Going to Get There?" instructions and clues (see appendix C) to the outside front of the large envelope.

2. Write or type the following on a three-by-five-inch index card: "You go through New Haven. 76 and 48 are exit numbers. 91 and 66 are route numbers."

3. Write or type "Open this if you are stumped" on the envelope; insert the card described above into the envelope, and tape it to the outside back of the large envelope.

4. Prepare six small envelopes as described below and place them inside the large envelope: On the outside of each envelope write or type one of the following combinations of route numbers:

138-52-2-3-91-99
1 38-52-2-16-66
138-95-9
3-1-95-81-9
138-95-77-17
138-95-91-66

In envelopes 1 through 5 insert a piece of paper that says, "Sorry. Try again."

5. In envelope 6 insert a piece of paper that says, "Congratulations! You are right!" Proceed to (location) for further instructions.

Envelope 4

1. Tape the "How Will We Know When We Are There?" instructions to the outside front of the large envelope.

2. Write or type the following on a three-by-five-inch index cards:

population

routes that go through the town

distances to nearby towns

the name of the college

3. Write or type "Open this if you are stumped" on a small letter envelope; insert the card described above into the envelope, and tape it to the outside back of the large envelope.

4. Place a blank sheet of paper inside the large envelope.

Appendix C

WHERE ARE WE NOW?

Use the clues given below and the atlas to determine the answer to this question. DO NOT OPEN THIS ENVELOPE UNTIL YOU HAVE DECIDED ON AN ANSWER. When you believe that you have the correct answer, open this envelope. Inside there are six small envelopes with possible answers written on them. Select the appropriate one and open it. If you are correct, the paper inside will tell you where to go to receive information about the next question. If you are wrong or if none of the envelopes has your answer written on it, determine which of the options is correct, using the clues given below. If at any point you are stumped, you may open the small envelope attached to the outside back of this envelope. The paper inside will give you further information that should enable you to reach a decision.

1. A road sign says, Norwich 20 miles

                         Kingston 12 miles

2. There is a road sign that is broken so that only the first part of the name of the town and the distance is readable. It says, Rock 2 miles.

3. It took three hours of traveling, averaging forty-five miles per hour, to arrive at the town you are in.

4. You did not travel the most direct route.

5. You can hear trucks going by at high speed.

6. The town you are in appears to be quite small, probably having not more than two thousand inhabitants.

7. The town is in a rural setting.

8. You don't appear to be close to the ocean.

WHERE DO WE WANT TO GO?

Use the clues given below and the atlas to determine the answer to this question. DO NOT OPEN THIS ENVELOPE UNTIL YOU HAVE DECIDED ON AN ANSWER. When you believe that you have the correct answer, open this envelope. Inside there are six small envelopes with answers written on them. Select the appropriate one and open it. If you are correct, the paper inside will tell you where to go to receive information about the next question. If you are wrong or if none of the envelopes has your answer written on it, determine which of the options is correct, using the clues given below. If at any point you are stumped, you may open the small envelope attached to the outside back of this envelope. The paper inside will give you further information that should enable you to reach a decision.

1. The end is in the middle.
2. A well, a field, a ham, and a dam are nearby.
3. In a connecting state.
4. Relatively large, but not among the biggest.
5. It's cap-and-gown territory.
6. Prehistoric evidence isn't far away.
7. The neighboring town is also found in Maine and Oregon.
8. In a river valley.

HOW ARE WE GOING TO GET THERE?

Use the clues given below and the atlas to determine the answer to this question. DO NOT OPEN THE LARGE ENVELOPE UNTIL YOU HAVE DECIDED ON AN ANSWER. When you believe that you have the correct answer, open this envelope. Inside there are six small envelopes with possible answers written on them. Select the appropriate one and open it. If you are correct, the paper inside will tell you where to go to receive information about the next question. If you are wrong or if none of the envelopes has your answer written on it, determine which of the options is correct, using the clues given below. If at any point you are stumped, you may open the small envelope attached to the outside back of this envelope. The paper inside will give you further information that should enable you to reach a decision.

1. The shortest isn't always right.
2. Route numbers are all that is needed.
3. Stick to the interstate.
4. The first leg is only one mile.
5. The westerly direction is south.
6. 76 is the right connection.
7. 28 on gold.
8. If you take 91 from 48, you'll get 66.
9. 390.

HOW WILL WE KNOW WHEN WE ARE THERE?

Use the clues you were given to determine "Where do we want to go?" as well as information from the atlas to develop specific descriptions that can be used to determine if you have arrived at your destination. These might begin with a statement such as, "We will see . . ." or "There will be . . ."

Example: If you had been told "A town of tall buildings," one description might be "We will see skyscrapers."

Write your descriptions of the destination on the sheet of paper enclosed in this envelope.

Appendix D

CREATIVE PLANNING

In many ways any planning we do is like taking a trip. The same questions that were considered during the simulation must be asked and answered in the planning process.

To plan creatively, we must answer these questions:

1. Where are we now?
2. Where do we want to go? (Or, what do we want to do?)
3. How are we going to get there? (Or, how are we going to do it?)
4. How will we know when we are there? (Or how will we know if we have done it?)

Now let's look at the work we did in the simulation and compare it to what happens in planning.

IN THE SIMULATION . . .	IN PLANNING . . .
We asked: Where are we now?	We ask: Where are we now?

The clues gave us information about:	We want to gather information about:
location setting	needs problems hopes
	We can do this by using:
	our own opinions or assumptions questionnaires or questions interviews observation

We used the clues and the atlas to determine:	When we have this information, we want to determine:
what area we were in what state we were in what town we were in	what needs/problems/hopes are common what needs/problems/hopes are most deeply felt what needs/problems/hopes we can do something about We can do this by: looking for things that keep repeating themselves seeing what coincides with our assumptions eliminating information that is not significant
Then—	Then—

We asked: Where do we want to go?	We ask: What do we want to do?

The clues gave us information about: state name nearby features	We want to: select the specific needs/problems/hopes to which we want to respond decide what it will be like when the response has been made
We used that information to determine our destination.	We can then describe that situation in a brief goal statement, which is: realistic—something we really can do specific—doesn't take in the whole world measurable—a change we can see
Then—	Then—

We asked: How are we going to get there?	We ask: How are we going to do it?
The clues gave us information about: 　　direction 　　route numbers	We want to decide: 　　who 　　does what 　　when
We used that information to put together the right combination of routes to reach our destination.	The best way to determine these strategies is to use a variety of creativity techniques to develop a list of possibilities; then select the best by asking: 　　Does this make the best use of 　　　our resources? 　　Is this workable in our 　　　situation? 　　Will this help us achieve our 　　　goal? Once the strategies have been decided upon, then the details for actually doing them need to be worked out.
Then—	Then—
We asked: How will we know when we are there?	We ask: How will we know if we have done it?
The clues that helped us answer "Where do we want to go?" gave us information about what our destination looked like.	We want to determine: 　　what indications there will be 　　　that the goal has been 　　　reached 　　what method(s) will be used 　　　to measure these indications

A method of deciding what the indications are is to look at the goal and ask, if this is achieved,

how will people act?
how will people feel?
what will people know?

The indications can be measured by use of:

observation
interviews (both formal and informal)
questionnaires

Then—	Then—
We had completed the game!	It is time to do it!

Option 2

The First Hour

1. Getting Back Together (10 minutes)

Discuss with your class what you observed during the "thumbs up-thumbs down" evaluation at the end of the last session. What did it tell you, the teacher? Did you make any changes in your session plan? Ask the group to share feelings and concerns they may have. Offer a prayer.

2. The Thirteen Teaching Steps (25 minutes)

Give each person a pair of scissors and cut out the teaching steps labels photocopied from page 44. After persons have completed the task, form groups of three and ask them to discuss the various steps. Which steps are most familiar? Place them in a pile. Which steps appear to be easiest? Place them in a pile. Which steps are new and unfamiliar? Place them in a separate pile. Share with others in the small group the "new and unfamiliar" pile.

3. Where Are We Now? (25 minutes)

Planning is like taking a trip. The first step in taking a trip is to know (or discover) where you are beginning. Steps 1-4 deal with the answers to the question, Where are we now? Refer them to printed prayers for their reading on pages 65, 72, and 79-80. Stress the importance of prayer. In small groups, ask them to work through what happened in the class they attended (or taught) last week and to make a list of concerns for that group (step 4).

Break (15 minutes)

The Second Hour

4. Where Do We Want to Go? (20 minutes)

Refer to page 48 and ask participants to read the definition of goals found there. Then refer them to the examples on page 49. Encourage each small group to take one of the concerns they listed above and practice writing a goal.

Refer to the first paragraph under "Step 6" on page 50. Suggest that they read and underline the last four sentences of that paragraph. Turn to page 51and point out that each objective begins with a time target. If time permits, ask them to try writing an objective.

5. How Are We Going to Get There? (25 minutes)

Begin by creating a session outline. Refer to information on page 52. In chapter 4, there are three illustrations of session plans. Select illustrations related to steps 8-10 you would like them to see and point them out to the participants; for example, see pages 67 and 68. Close this section by briefly discussing step 11—participation. Stress its importance.

6. How Will We Know When We Are There? (10 minutes)

Point out the evaluation questions on pages 57 and 58. Ask participants to evaluate this session on the basis of those questions. What would they have done differently if they had prepared this session? Encourage clear feedback.

7. Closure (5 minutes)

Assign chapter 4 to be read for the next session. Close with prayer.

Session 4: Teaching Activities (Chapter 4)

Chapter 4 presents three different methods of teaching with a full session plan for each method. Each of the three methods deals with a different age level. As the teacher, you will be a resource person for all class members, who probably represent different age-level interests. Therefore you should be familiar with the different methods offered by each model.

The exercises provided in this guide will be more beneficial if you divide the total group into age-level small groups. Those persons interested in teaching children can be placed in one group, as can those interested in youth and adult age levels.

Session 4 Objectives

The following objectives will be accomplished by the end of this session.

1. Students will experience the thirteen steps of the session-planning process while using curriculum materials.

2. Students will be able to apply the session-planning steps to their own preparation for teaching.

3. Students will discover a large number of teaching activities/methods for the age level in which they teach or have an interest.

The First Hour

1. Review Feedback on the Simulation Game (15 minutes)

Ask participants to share with the total group what they wrote on the three-by-five-inch cards about the simulation game experienced in session 3. Guide them in sharing their feelings about the experience. Was the simulation game a helpful learning experience? What did they learn from it? If you used option 2, review the last session.

2. Brainstorm Teaching Methods (20 minutes)

Divide the total group into three age-level small groups, including children, youth, and adult. If only one person expresses interest in one of the age levels, shift that person to one of the other groups or work with that person on an individual basis while the others work in two small groups.

Ask each group to prepare a list of teaching methods/activities that would be suitable for their age-level interest. For instance, the group of teachers interested in children's classes would focus on methods of teaching for children. Suggest that they may want to check back to Dale's Cone of Learning for some guidance and ideas (page 31). Each group should prepare its list on newsprint (if available) for presentation to the total group. After ten minutes of work together, ask each group to share with the total group the list they have compiled.

3. Begin to Apply Session Planning Steps to Curriculum Material (25 minutes)

Ask them to get out the curriculum materials they brought. Also ask them to get the cutout labels from session 3 ready for use. For the rest of session 4, it will be best if participants work in pairs. If the number of participants is not even, there can be one group of three persons.

Participants from other churches probably will bring different curriculum materials. This can happen within a church also. It will take some time, but if it is possible, match teachers who use the same curriculum material.

Ask them to select one session with which to use the step-by-step planning process from session 3. They will need time to review the material and make their selection. When they have selected the session, it will most likely be time for a break.

Break (10-15 minutes)

The Second Hour

4. Use Session-Planning Steps (45 minutes)

Using their cutout labels as a guide, have the participants work through the session step by step. Encourage them to ask for help if they need it. You should be available to all of the pairs of small groups. Check in with each pair from time to time to encourage them and to observe progress.

Look Ahead to Session 5 (10 minutes)

Ask the group if there are areas of concerns that they would like to deal with in the last session. Receive suggestions from the group. You might want to be prepared with a brief overview of what you will be dealing with if they do not have suggestions. Assign chapter 5 for outside reading.

6. *Closure* (5 minutes)

Place a sheet of newsprint on a wall near the door. Ask participants to evaluate this session using colors. Have crayons available near the newsprint. A color code might include:

Blue: I feel great about session planning.

Brown: I have average or "so-so" feelings.

Red: I feel frustrated about session planning.

Ask each person to draw a mark or design on the newsprint as he or she leaves, which reflects his or her feelings about session planning.

Form a circle and close with sentence prayers for each other.

Session 5: Teacher Growth, Plus Some Concluding Points (Chapter 5)

Session 5 Objectives

1. By the time they leave this session, students will receive answers and guidance to their most urgent questions and concerns.

2. Teachers will make a commitment to teacher growth by the end of the session.

3. By the end of this session, each student will provide an evaluation of the course.

4. Instructor and students will celebrate their learning together by the end of the session.

The First Hour

1. Concerns from Session 4 (20 minutes or whatever time is needed)

You may or may not have produced a list of concerns from session 4. The opportunity was given for students to indicate areas they would like you to address in the last session. Use your best judgment as to how to respond to the list. If no list was generated, move ahead to the second step of this first hour after some discussion of section 4.

2. Teacher Growth (40 minutes)

Begin by asking the students to turn to the basic teacher role form they filled out in chapter 2 (page 27). As they conclude this course of study, how do they feel about the roles described in chapter 2? Did you discover any clues in what they said about themselves with which to begin to design steps for teacher growth?

Are there other teacher growth areas in which they have interest? These could include, for example, teaching activities, age-level characteristics, Bible knowledge, etc. Help them discover where to begin.

Suggest that each person list the areas of teacher growth in which he or she has an interest and then prioritize the list. Which area of teacher growth ranks number one? Which is second, and so on? After each person has identified his or her top priority, ask each to share it with the class. Ask the class to make suggestions about how and where this learning could be secured. Ask the class to serve as a resource bank of ideas for each student.

Depending on the size of your class, forty minutes may or may not be sufficient to complete this exercise. It is very important that every student have an opportunity to share his or her top priority for growth. Be sure to take the necessary time to include everyone in the process.

Break (10-15 minutes)

Refreshments could be provided at this time rather than at the close of the session. If participants have some distance to travel, refreshments would be more suitable now.

The Second Hour

3. Home Visitation (20 minutes)

It is important that new teachers understand the importance of home visitation. It is also important for them to know how to make a home contact successfully. Role play several visits with your students taking different parts. Create situations with children, youth, and adults who are contacted. Stop the role play at various points to illustrate what has been learned.

4. Evaluation (20 minutes)

For this evaluation exercise, divide your class into groups of three, four, or five persons. Provide each group with a balloon and a broad felt-tip marker. Have each group blow up its balloon as a group experience. Encourage group members to "contribute" some "hot air" to their balloons.

After it is blown up to a good size, write on it with the marker. Provide questions with which students can evaluate the course; for example: What is the most important thing you learned in the course? How do you feel about the course? Did the course provide you with the tools you need to teach? Encourage each person to write different reactions, feelings, and observations about the course on the balloon. Encourage each student to share with others in small groups the meaning that lies behind what has been written.

5. *Looking Ahead* (20 minutes)

Bring the small groups together. Place the balloons on the floor or on a table in the middle of the group. Give a five-minute inspirational talk or devotional. Encourage them to share their hopes, dreams, concerns, and goals as they look to their teaching future. Close the evening with a prayer circle, and use sentence prayers to pray for each other, reflecting on what has just been shared.